Management Arrangements for the Reorganised National Health Service

© *Crown copyright 1972*

SBN 11 320485 X

MEMBERSHIP OF THE MANAGEMENT STUDY STEERING COMMITTEE

Chairman: Sir Philip Rogers KCB CMG

Members:

Non-Departmental

C E Astley Esq MD MB ChB FRCP
Miss E A Bell SRN SCM RNMS RMPA
P M Cooke Esq MA FHA MRSH   Co-opted December 1971
G Cumming Esq BSc PhD DSc MB ChB
FRIC FRCP
Miss M I Farrer OBE DN(Lond) SRN SCM
MTD
Miss E Few SRN HV(Cert) NDN Cert
(Queen's Nurse) RCN Admin Cert (Public
Health)
C W Gordon Esq TD MB ChB FRCP FFCM
DPH DRPH
Dame Isabel Graham Bryce DBE MA
Professor E Jaques MA MD PhD FPsych
S Ludkin Esq MD BS FFCM DPH
J H Marks Esq MB ChB(Edin) MRCGP
D(Obst) RCOG
*Sir Richard Meyjes   Resigned March 1972
*W M Naylor Esq BA FHA JP
J N Peacock Esq CBE FDSRCS
Professor P Rhodes FRCS FRCOG
A B Scott Esq OBE MA FHA
R C Sharphouse Esq FIMTA FHA
*S H A Shaw Esq LLB FCIS FHA JP
Miss B Smith SRN SCM
C C Stevens Esq OBE LLB FPS
R R Thornton Esq MA LLB
C J Wells Esq OBE TD MB ChB MRCGP

Department of Health and Social Security

E B S Alton Esq MBE MC
C L Bourton Esq   Appointed June 1972
*D H D Burbridge Esq OBE MRCS FFCM
DPH
A J Collier Esq
J P Dodds Esq CB
Miss P M Friend CBE SRN SCM   Appointed May 1972
R Gedling Esq CB   Appointed November 1971
G D Gibb Esq LDSRCS   Appointed January 1972
Surg R/Admiral W Holgate CB OBE
FDSRCS   Resigned December 1971
F W Mottershead Esq CB   Resigned September 1971

3

J S Orme Esq CB OBE   Resigned June 1972
Dame Kathleen Raven DBE SRN SCM   Resigned April 1972
H C Salter Esq DFC   Resigned May 1972
K R Stowe Esq
W G Wilson Esq OBE   Appointed June 1972
H Yellowlees Esq CB MA BM BCh MRCS
FRCP FFCM

Secretary
  *E Caines Esq
*Also member of the Study Group

STUDY GROUP

Chairman: F D K Williams Esq Department of Health and Social Security
Members (in addition to the members of the Steering Committee indicated with
    an asterisk):

Non-Departmental
  A Allen Esq ACIS
  H W S Francis Esq MA MB BChir FFCM DPH
  Miss M R Worster SRN

Department of Health and Social Security
  S Bayfield Esq
  N J B Evans Esq MA MB BChir MRCP DPH Barrister at Law
  H G Jones Esq
  L G S Mason Esq OBE
  R S Matthews Esq
  Miss J G Whitehead SRN SCM

Secretary
  F V Rees Esq

The Study Group had the assistance of management consultants from McKinsey
& Co Inc. and of the Health Services Organisation Research Unit of Brunel
University under Professor Jaques.

4

CONTENTS

FOREWORD

1. This report proposes management arrangements for the reorganised National Health Service which will now be considered by the Secretary of State for Social Services in consultation with the interests concerned. These proposals are the outcome of a study supervised by a Steering Committee, with membership drawn almost entirely from the three branches of the present NHS and from the Department, with the following terms of reference:

"On the basis of the Government's Consultative Document on National Health Service reorganisation, and taking account of other relevant studies commissioned by the Secretary of State, to make recommendations on management systems for the services for which Regional and Area Health Authorities will be responsible and on the internal organisation of those Authorities."

2. The Study was required to take account of the present arrangements for the administration of the individual parts of the NHS and of current developments in the organisation of the work of the medical, nursing and other relevant professions.

3. The study has been conducted in the setting of the Government's decisions on the future organisation of the National Health Service as set out in the White Paper "National Health Service Reorganisation: England" (Cmnd 5055). Account has also been taken of work being done in other relevant fields. This includes the Working Party on Medical Administrators; the Working Party on Collaboration between the new health authorities and local government, and the review of the organisation and operation of the Central Department.

4. The study concentrated on the Regional Health Authorities, Area Health Authorities and their Districts, and Family Practitioner Committees and has resulted in the further definition of functions of Regional and Area Health Authorities and of the relationships between them, and in proposed arrangements for their internal organisation and processes. The composition and functions of the Community Health Councils were not examined, since this was covered by the White Paper.

5. No distinction is made in the report between arrangements in respect of which there will need to be national uniformity and those which should be left to the option of the Authorities concerned.

6. Preliminary proposals were the subject of detailed discussion in particular areas (Berkshire, Doncaster, Hillingdon, Lambeth/Southwark, Lincolnshire, Nottinghamshire and Oxfordshire). These were selected as being representative of the local variations of circumstances likely to arise. In each area discussions took place with local professional and multi-disciplinary groups to identify the main problems and to see how the proposals might be applied to real situations. The study has been much helped by these discussions, by preliminary discussions in a number of other places and by constructive thinking that has been taking place generally. The application to particular areas and especially to large densely populated urban areas will have to be the subject of detailed local study. Acknowledgement is due to the many people who have contributed much time and effort to this work.

7.   In this report particular words have been used in a precise management sense. These are defined on the first page of Appendix 3.

8.   The Steering Committee accepts that certain of the management arrangements have inevitably been determined by decisions which the Secretary of State has taken on the basis of his own independent consultations with other bodies. The management arrangements recommended in this report have been agreed by the Steering Committee after detailed discussion, though not every member of the Steering Committee would have wished every detail of the proposals to be precisely as formulated. With these qualifications, the conclusions of this study command the full support of all the members of the Steering Committee.

9.   Before reaching and announcing conclusions on the proposals the Secretary of State will consult the management, professional and staff interests concerned.

CHAPTER 1
ENDS AND MEANS

1.1. The objective in reorganising the National Health Service (NHS) is to enable health care to be improved. Success in achieving this objective depends primarily on the people in the health care professions who prevent, diagnose and treat disease. Management plays only a subsidiary part, but the way in which the Service is organised and the processes used in directing resources can help or hinder the people who play the primary part. This Chapter sets out first, the framework, aims and principles underlying the proposed arrangements; and second, six features of the arrangements which will be especially important in helping to achieve the objective.

A. FRAMEWORK, AIMS AND PRINCIPLES

(1) Framework

1.2. The management arrangements have been designed to fit the organisational framework described in the White Paper. The following are important features of this framework:

a. There are to be Area Health Authorities (AHA)—including some Area Health Authorities (Teaching) (AHA(T)) with particular medical and dental teaching responsibilities—accountable to Regional Health Authorities (RHA), who are in turn to be accountable to the Secretary of State for the effectiveness and efficiency of the services provided.

b. These AHAs are to be coterminous geographically with the new local authorities (counties and metropolitan districts) which are to be set up outside London, and with the present London Boroughs or combinations of London Boroughs.

c. Each AHA is to be required by statute to set up a Family Practitioner Committee (FPC) to administer the contracts of practitioners.

d. There is to be statutory provision for the recognition of professional advisory machinery from which RHAs, AHAs and FPCs will draw advice.

e. Community Health Councils (CHC) are to be established to represent the views of the public to the AHAs.

(2) Aims

1.3. The starting point of the study was an appreciation of the reasons why reorganisation had been decided upon, in order to determine what features should be built into the new structure to obtain the benefits which reorganisation is expected to bring.

1.4. The general aims in reorganisation are first, that there should be a fully integrated Health Service in which every aspect of health care can be provided by members of the health-care professions and second, that this care should be provided so far as possible locally and with due regard to the health needs of the community as a whole. Within these general aims there are some more specific objectives which the management arrangements ought to promote:

a. Co-ordination of the planning and provision of all personal health services (including health education, prevention, diagnosis, treatment and rehabilitation) with each other and with local government services.*
b. Planning of services in relation to needs of the people to be served (e.g. the elderly, the mentally ill, the physically handicapped) irrespective of whether the services are provided in the home, in the doctor's surgery or in hospital.
c. The more effective working of professional practitioners through the provision of a structure and systems to support them administratively.
d. Means whereby doctors and dentists can contribute more effectively to NHS decision making.
e. More uniform national standards of care.
f. Innovation and the rapid implementation of improved approaches to health care.
g. Clear, but flexible career structures for staff.
h. Effective education and training of Health Service personnel.

Education is mentioned frequently in this report. The continuing education and training of all staff are essential features of an effective Service, for the best health care depends on sound research followed by the diffusion of results through education.

(3) Principles

1.5. In proposing management arrangements some general organisational principles have been followed. These principles have been derived both from study of the Consultative Document and from reflection on the nature of the NHS:

a. The health-care professions should be integrally involved in planning and management at all levels. This involvement must be achieved without infringing the clinical autonomy of medical and dental consultants and general practitioners and without interfering with the professional standards of the health-care professions or inhibiting the exercise of professional judgement by members of those professions.
b. Responsibilities must be clearly defined and allocated. This applies both to the responsibilities of RHAs and AHAs and the relationships between them and to the responsibilities of officers of RHAs and AHAs and their decision-making discretion. It should be clearly established for what duties an officer will be accountable and to whom.
c. There should be maximum decentralisation and delegation of decision making, but within policies established at national, Regional and Area levels.
d. Higher organisation must be designed to provide policies within which local services can be managed effectively. Higher levels of management should therefore agree objectives with lower levels as the basis for delegating authority and for monitoring performance.
e. Delegation downwards should be matched with accountability upwards.

* Although the Industrial Medical Service is not to be part of the NHS close liaison between the two Services will be necessary.

B. SIX KEY FEATURES

1.6. Three of the six key features in the new arrangements relate directly to the aims of reorganisation set out in paragraph 1.3:

(1) It is proposed that health services be integrated locally, within Areas, on a "district" basis, since many areas will be too large to form effective operational units.

(2) In a patient-centred approach to health care it is essential that there should be active participation by clinicians in management, particularly at the operational level. It is proposed that clinicians should participate through representative committees with elected spokesmen.

(3) To achieve integration, it is proposed that multi-disciplinary management teams be formed at each level to plan and co-ordinate health services jointly.

1.7. Two of the key features relate to the principles set out in paragraph 1.5:

(4) Responsibilities must be clearly allocated and defined—the respective roles of the members of an Authority and its officers, the relation of the RHA to its AHAs and the authority of managers over their subordinates.

(5) Decentralisation of decision making, implicit in the patient-centred approach, can be balanced with the need for national and Regional strategic direction by means of a planning system.

1.8. The sixth key feature is related to the constraint set by the framework described in paragraph 1.2:

(6) The arrangements must be flexible, to allow for adaptation to particular situations. For example, there is great variation in the size of Areas and Regions, so that the ways of achieving economies of scale will also vary.

1.9. The rest of this Chapter describes successively each of these six key features.

(1) Integration at District level

1.10. The determining factor in constituting Areas is the need to establish effective planning links with the matching local authorities, which will provide complementary services. In consequence, there will be great variety in the size of Areas. It is clear that comprehensive integration of health services should be sought at Area level, but this should not exclude comprehensive integration at lower levels if a "natural" level for it can be established. The approach has been to start with the patient and work up, identifying the various points at which integration takes place.*

1.11. The primary operational element is the general medical practitioner. He may have, on average, about 2,500 people on his list. There is an instance

---

*The analysis relates to the future rather than to the existing pattern of primary and hospital care and anticipates wider development of district general hospitals, health centres and primary-care teams.

of integration each time a general practitioner refers his patient to a consultant specialist or prescribes treatment to be carried out, for example, by a home nurse (presently employed by the local authority). A different form of integration also occurs when the general practitioner provides various preventive services, such as immunisation or screening, or works in the school health service, which are at present the responsibility of the local authority. These instances of integration all relate to individual members of the public and to individual health-care practitioners.

1.12. The first example of more formal organisational integration is the formation of group practices, when, for example, 5 general practitioners work together to serve, say, 12,500 people. Twenty percent of general practitioners at present work single-handed although the proportion has been decreasing steadily. The present mean size of group practice is 3, but 15 percent of general practitioners now work in groups of 5 or more, and the trend is towards larger groups. Further structural integration takes place with the development of a "primary-care team"—one or two group practices (perhaps 10 general practitioners) with an attached team of health visitors and home nurses, practising from a health centre or the general practitioners' own purpose-built premises. This primary-care team might serve 15,000 to 25,000 people, with an upper limit of perhaps 30,000 people.

1.13. Serving complementary social needs there will be the social workers of the local authority. They will normally be organised in family-centred, "area" social work teams of around 10 social workers, serving 50,000 to 60,000 people. In theory therefore, these social work teams will be complementary to two primary-care teams, and it should be possible by reorganisation to achieve effective integration between health and social services at this level. For example, the siting of health centres and the planning of social work areas could be co-ordinated so as to achieve matching responsibilities. In addition, the community nursing organisation might include a post for a nursing manager who could co-ordinate her activities with those of the "area" social work team leaders.

1.14. A community of around 200,000 to 300,000 is about the smallest for which substantially the full range of general health and social services can be provided. At this level the primary-care teams can be supported by the specialist services of the district general hospital. For example, on average, a population of 250,000 may be served by (among others) 5 consultants in general medicine, 5 consultants in general surgery, 6 consultant psychiatrists, 3 consultants in gynaecology and obstetrics, 2 paediatricians, 1 geriatrician and 1 dental surgeon. These consultants practise from and use the resources of the district general hospital or the group of hospitals which provides a district service. Consultants and general practitioners will tend to establish contact at this level both for patient referrals and for domiciliary consultations. Often the Area will coincide with such a "natural" district, in which case integration with local authority policy making will occur at this level, but many Areas will include between two and five such districts.

1.15. It is proposed therefore that the District—defined as a population served by community health services supported by the specialist services of a district general hospital—should be the basic operational unit of the integrated Health Service. Three further arguments point to this conclusion:

a. The benefits of integration will be achieved largely as the result of the new opportunity created to plan comprehensively, in the sense of reviewing and modifying operational policies and methods and re-allocating resources in relation to needs.
b. To be effective, such planning must be responsive to the specific needs of the local community, and must take account of the available resources and existing levels of provision and of innovation at the operational level, and it must reflect what is practical and acceptable in the opinion of local professional practitioners.
c. The District is the largest-sized unit within which consultants, general practitioners and others can participate actively in the management process through effective representative systems.

1.16. The following figures broadly indicate current experience and hence the size of the task in a District of 250,000 population:

a. There might for example be 60,000 children, of whom 500 might be physically handicapped and 200 mentally handicapped.
b. There might be 35,000 people over 65, of whom 4,500 might be physically handicapped. 800 old people might be in hospital, 800 in old people's homes, and 1,000 might be living at home alone and requiring domiciliary care.
c. There might be in all age groups 7,000 severely physically-handicapped people.
d. There might be 700 mentally-handicapped people, of whom 350 might be in hospital.
e. There might be 2,500 mentally-ill people of all ages, in contact with hospitals and 580 of these might be inpatients.
f. 19,000 people might require acute medical or surgical care each year as inpatients, of whom 550 might be in hospital at one point in time.

1.17.   Chapter 2 shows how the existing three parts of the Health Service can be integrated within Districts, describes the functions to be delegated to District management and introduces the "District Management Team" (DMT), responsible for planning and providing integrated care within a District. It will be necessary to define these Districts geographically, and since the natural health districts will not usually fall exactly within county or metropolitan district boundaries, it will be necessary to make arrangements for cases where there is an overlap. The arrangements for the definition of Districts and for overlap problems are described in Appendix 1.

(2) Participation of clinicians

1.18.   The management arrangements required for the NHS are different from those commonly used in other large organisations because the work is different. The distinguishing characteristic of the NHS is that to do their work properly, consultants and general practitioners* must have clinical autonomy, so that they can be fully responsible for the treatment they prescribe for their patients. It follows that these doctors and dentists work as each others' equals

* This term is used to include dentists as well as doctors.

13

and that they are their own managers. In ethics and in law they are accountable to their patients for the care they prescribe, and they cannot be held accountable to the NHS Authorities for the quality of their clinical judgements so long as they act within the broad limits of acceptable medical practice and within policy for the use of resources.

1.19. The essential task of management in the Health Service is to organise limited resources—human, financial and physical—so as to enable the community to be provided with the best possible standard and balance of care. This entails establishing priorities between conflicting claims. The demands which are made on resources by clinicians in providing care have to be reconciled one with another. The actions of clinicians also interact in complex ways with the work of other people in the Health Service and personal social services. Also, clinicians are an important source of innovation, in both medical practice and general approaches to care, and their ideas must be evaluated—and, where appropriate, translated into action by management.

1.20. Clinicians should therefore participate in the management process so that they can bring to management accurate and up-to-date knowledge of the clinical situation and contribute to decisions on priorities; commit themselves to agreed proposals for change and obtain a full understanding of the impact of their work on other parts of the Service. To be effective, this medical involvement must not be intermittent but should be a systematic part of the Service. The appropriate form of participation is the respresentative committee, through which clinicians can regulate their own activities. These committees will be consensus-forming groups, whose decisions should be binding on their members. The consensus of the committees will be represented by elected spokesmen who must be able to speak for their colleagues.

1.21. It is therefore proposed to arrange ways in which clinicians can participate, either directly or through their elected representatives, in decisions about the way local health services should develop:

a. *Individual clinicians* will participate directly within Districts as members of health-care planning teams (see paragraph 1.24) in developing proposals for improving local services in their particular speciality or sphere of interest.
b. *Elected Representatives* of general practitioners and consultants will be members of DMTs, which will have substantial authority delegated to them by the AHA.
c. *Professional advisory committees* are to be established for RHAs and AHAs, and these will be consulted before the important planning and allocation decisions are made.

Thus, clinicians will be actively involved both at the stage when plans are formulated and when decisions are made at the local level. They will also participate through professional advisory committees, whose recognition is to be a statutory requirement. Chapter 4 in Part II of this report describes in more detail the role of doctors in management.

14

(3) Co-ordination by multi-disciplinary teams

1.22. A characteristic of the Health Service is that the provision of health care is often a team activity. Different skills have to be combined in various ways to meet the needs of individual patients; different professions must come together to plan and co-ordinate their activities to meet complex objectives; and the work of the various skill groups has to be co-ordinated within institutions.

1.23. Management in the health services can be regarded as having three dimensions: (i) the *needs* of people for various forms of health care ("health-care groups"* as they have been called in this report); (ii) the *skills* of the people who meet the needs; and (iii) the *places* where care is given. The three dimensions are illustrated in Exhibit I.

1.24. Because of this complexity, organisation in a single hierarchy controlled by a chief executive is not appropriate. The appropriate structure is based on unified management within the hierarchically-organised professions, on representative systems within the non-hierarchically organised medical and dental professions, and on co-ordination *between* professions. Co-ordination between professions at all levels will be achieved by multi-disciplinary teams through which the managers and representatives of the relevant professions can jointly make decisions. Such teams co-ordinate activities within institutions and Districts, co-ordinate the planning of services directed to meet the needs of health-care groups and co-ordinate decision making at each of three levels of management—District, Area and Region.

1.25. The constitution of each of the teams in the third category is described in Section II of Chapter 2, but they have the following common characteristics. The teams will be consensus bodies, that is, decisions will need the agreement of each of the team members. They will share joint responsibility to the Authority for preparing plans, making delegated planning and operational decisions, and monitoring performance against plans. The teams must be small, and will therefore consist only of those whose unanimous agreement is essential to the making and effective implementation of decisions for the totality of health care. To fulfil these two conditions team members must be either elected representatives of clinicians or managers of their professions directly accountable to the Authority, and also be concerned with the whole range of the decisions to be made by the team. In addition to being responsible jointly as members of the team, officers in these teams will also be accountable individually for the performance of specific functions.

1.26. At each level there will also be heads of some professions directly accountable to the Authority and not subordinate to a team member, but not concerned with the whole range of team decisions. These officers will not be team members and their work will be co-ordinated with the general programme of activities by one of the team members. They will, however, receive agendas, papers and minutes and have the right to attend team meetings and to participate in discussions affecting their services.

---

* This replaces the expression "patient groups" as used in the Appendix on management arrangements published in the White Paper.

EXHIBIT I

**District organisation can be
regarded in terms of a
3—dimensional model . . . .**

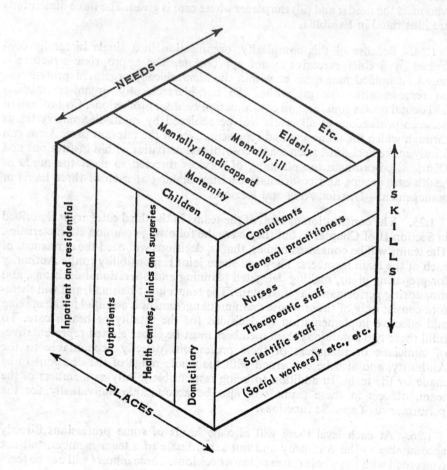

NEEDS

Etc.

Elderly

Mentally ill

Mentally handicapped

Maternity

Children

SKILLS

Consultants

General practitioners

Nurses

Therapeutic staff

Scientific staff

(Social workers)* etc., etc.

Inpatient and residential

Outpatients

Health centres, clinics and surgeries

Domiciliary

PLACES

*   *Employed outside the NHS*

1.27. The team being made up of equals, each member will co-ordinate the team on matters of particular relevance to his own discipline ("functional co-ordination"). However, it is necessary to ensure that no team becomes ineffective through failure to initiate ideas or lack of drive to carry them through. An Authority will therefore need to provide more formally for chairmanship of a team. Such a chairman should either be elected by the team subject to the approval of the Authority or appointed by the Authority after such consultation with the team as the Authority thinks fit. The choice between the two alternatives will be for decision by the Authority. The team chairman may be any member of the team. He will formally take the chair at meetings, but discussion on particular topics will be led by the team member with the principal interest in the matter under consideration. The chairman's leadership will be exercised not only at meetings so as to get the necessary decisions taken, but also between meetings to stimulate action. The role, if not falling to an administrator, will need to be exercised in close co-operation with him, drawing on the services of his department. This administrator, who will be a member of the team at each level, will provide administrative support for the other members of the team in their co-ordinative roles and have included in his role tasks of general administrative co-ordination to ensure that the total programme is co-ordinated in its planning and development.

(4) Clear allocation of authority and accountability

1.28. Accountability in the Health Service is not easily determined, because consultants and general practitioners are primarily accountable to their patients. However, except for consultants and general practitioners, the other professions, and indeed, doctors in medical administration, can suitably be organised in managerial hierarchies, and the effective provision of health care will thus depend to a considerable extent on the effectiveness of many thousands of managers. These managers must be held accountable not only for their own work but also for the work of their subordinates. In order to carry this accountability, the authority of managers must be made clear and it must carry with it the right to have immediate subordinates who are capable of doing the work required. The manager must therefore be able to decide how he delegates the work; he must assess the performance of subordinates; and, to the extent that he is required to have or retain subordinates who cannot do what is necessary, he cannot be held fully accountable for their performance. Policies and procedures will therefore have to be developed for improving the opportunities for transfer of personnel into posts where they may make their best contribution.

1.29. Managers must also have authority clearly delegated to them by the statutory Authority. The distribution of responsibilities between the Members of RHAs and AHAs and their officers is described in Chapter 2. It is based on the following principles: (i) Members of Authorities should devote their limited time to major issues of policy planning and resource allocation; (ii) Authorities should require their officers to present them with argued and supported alternatives with the major issues requiring their consideration; (iii) officers should have executive authority to implement policies and plans delegated to them after agreeing with the Authority specific targets and measures of performance; (iv) the Authority should monitor and control performance in relation to the agreed measures of performance.

1.30. For each officer in management there must be a role specification, describing the purpose of his position, the principal responsibilities and the main working relationships, showing to whom he is accountable, whom he manages directly, whom he monitors and co-ordinates or is monitored or co-ordinated by. Examples for new posts are shown in Appendix 3 to Part II of this report. The role specification for a given post should be prepared by the officer who is going to fill the post and agreed with his immediate superior. It should be updated every year, and published within the organisation so that everyone knows who is responsible to whom and for what.

(5) Decentralisation balanced with strategic direction

1.31. The need to decentralise local planning and operational responsibilities must be balanced against the need for national and Regional strategic direction and control over public funds. This will be achieved by means of a comprehensive and formal planning and monitoring process. The word "planning" is here used to refer to the process of deciding in what way the future should be better than the present, what changes are necessary to bring about these improvements, and how these changes can be implemented. As such, planning is nothing new to the NHS, and what is proposed here is not a new departure, but rather a development of existing procedures into a more comprehensive process, covering the total health-care needs of the community and all the health services to be provided to meet these needs. In particular:

  a. Explicit plans will be prepared for each District, that cover the whole range of its community's needs for health care, and the whole range of health services to be provided to meet these needs, for a period up to 10 years ahead, and focusing not only on the new building required, but on all the resources needed to achieve the objectives.
  b. This systematic planning process will be in the form of an interactive dialogue between DHSS, RHAs and AHAs and their District managements, in which the main management control exercised by one level over another is the allocation of resources and the setting of guidelines to the level below, followed by review and approval of their plans. Once these have been agreed, operating authority can be delegated and accountability will be effected through monitoring performance in relation to agreed plans.
  c. Responsibility for making planning proposals will be placed on the teams at District, Area and Regional levels (see paragraphs 1.25–1.27), who will be supported by the information and planning functions of the AHA and RHA.

1.32. Once the planning proposals have been approved, the District management, the AHA and the RHA will have delegated authority to implement them. To maintain accountability upwards in each case, their performance will be monitored and controlled in relation to these plans by the next higher Authority.

(6) The need for flexibility

1.32. There will be variety in the size of Areas and Regions (see Exhibit II), in the problems facing managers and in the calibre of managers. The arrangements must therefore be adaptable to local situations, while conforming with

EXHIBIT II

REGIONS AND AREAS VARY IN SIZE

Regions	Population of Region	Number of Areas	NUMBER OF AREAS IN POPULATION BRACKETS				
			Under 250,000	250,000 to 500,000	500,000 to 750,000	750,000 to 1,000,000	Over 1,000,000
	(000's)						
Birmingham	5.105	11	1	7	1	1	1
Sheffield	4.283	8	2	1	2	3	—
Manchester	4.107	11	5	4	1	—	1
Leeds	3.501	7	1	3	2	1	—
Newcastle	3.139	9	3	4	2	—	—
South Western	3.024	5	—	3	—	2	—
Wessex	2.518	3	—	1	1	—	1
Liverpool	2.471	6	2	2	1	1	—
Oxford	2.074	6	2	2	1	1	—
East Anglia	1.697	3	—	—	3	—	—
North East Met*	—	1*	—	—	—	—	1
South East Met*	—	2*	—	—	1	—	1
South West Met*	—	2*	—	—	1	1	—
North West Met*	—	2*	—	1	—	1	—
TOTAL		76	16	28	16	11	5

* Non-London areas only. The four metropolitan regions will include London AHA's. These have yet to be decided and are not included in this analysis.

organisational principles that can be applied throughout the NHS. The necessary flexibility is built into the proposed arrangements in a number of ways.

   a. *Within Districts*, a number of alternative arrangements are suggested, to fit different circumstances, using the same organisational concepts but applying them in different combinations.
   b. *Within Areas*, it will be necessary, in the first instance, to decide how many Districts to establish. The "district" concept is itself a means of dealing with the diversity in size of Areas, the larger Areas needing more Districts. Thus, with the District as a module, the arrangements proposed will be suitable to the whole range of circumstances, from the small Area with around 200,000 population to the large Area with over a million.
   c. *Within Regions*, it will be possible to decide which services are most efficiently provided by the various AHAs and which by the RHA, important considerations being the size of each Area and its competence in relation to particular functions.

1.33. These six key features recur at different points in the remainder of this report: in Part I, which outlines the proposals for organisation (Chapter 2) and processes (Chapter 3); and in Part II, which describes more particularly the proposed organisation in one of the three dimensions of management, skill groups.

19

Part I
Outline of Arrangements

CHAPTER 2
ORGANISATION

2.1. This Chapter is in two sections. The first describes the allocation of functions between the statutory Authorities and their officers. The second describes the organisational arrangements proposed at each level for achieving co-ordination in the planning and provision of health care and managing the service. The proposals incorporate the key features introduced in Chapter 1.

Section I—Distribution of Functions

2.2. The relationship between the three levels of statutory Authority—the Secretary of State, RHA and AHA—is to be established by Parliament in legislation. It is one of delegation from the Secretary of State to RHA and from RHA to AHA, with corresponding accountability upwards. The exact distribution of functions between levels will not be fixed in legislation. The aim will be to effect the greatest possible decentralisation and delegation from the Secretary of State to RHA, and from RHA to AHA. The allocation of functions set out in this Chapter should therefore be considered as the normal, but not in all respects the invariable, position.

2.3. The distribution of functions is described in three parts:
a. The functions of the AHA, and their allocation between the Authority and its officers at Area headquarters and in District management.
b. The functions of the RHA, and their allocation between the Authority and its officers.
c. The functions of the Secretary of State and the Department of Health and Social Security (DHSS).

A. FUNCTIONS OF THE AREA HEALTH AUTHORITY

2.4. The AHA is the lowest level of statutory Authority, with full planning and operational responsibilities. It will be responsible for providing or arranging for the provision of comprehensive health services to the people of its Area. To provide the best possible balance of care it will determine its policies and plan its services in conjunction with the matching local authorities, through statutory joint consultative committees. The AHA will plan services, establish priorities and allocate resources to operational services in relation to the specific needs of the community served, within national and Regional policy guidelines and the resources allocated to it by the RHA. It will be held accountable to the RHA for the operational control of its services. In addition it will employ staff working in the Area*, and will make arrangements with independent contractors

* But the RHA will employ consultants and senior registrars, except in AHA(T)s.

for the provision by them of general medical, dental, ophthalmic and pharmaceutical services. Certain types of capital building projects will be delegated to the AHA in relation to its capabilities.*

2.5.   An AHA(T) will have special responsibilities for providing facilities in support of medical and dental teaching carried out by the Universities, and in support of associated research.

2.6.   The AHA will be statutorily required to establish a Family Practitioner Committee (FPC) to carry out certain prescribed functions in relation to the administration of contracts for services. The four functions of the FPC will be to enter into contracts for services with practitioners and other persons (e.g. chemist contractors); to prepare lists of such practitioners and other persons, under regulations; to pay such practitioners and other persons the sums due to them under their contracts for services; and to deal with disputes and complaints arising out of the performance of their contracts by practitioners. The statutory responsibilities of the FPC will not, however, include other functions which, although related to the family practitioner services, will be carried out by the AHA. These include planning and organisation of family practitioner services, e.g. the development of health centres and arranging schemes for attaching nurses and other staff to general practitioners. The AHA will, however, consult the FPC before deciding on these matters.

2.7.   The following paragraphs describe the role of the AHA and its Members and of the officers at Area headquarters and in District Management Teams (DMTs). This distribution of functions has been designed in accordance with the features described in Chapter 1. The aim has been to reflect, on the one hand, the need to integrate services at the District level and to achieve the maximum possible delegation to that level, and, on the other hand, the need to plan jointly with the local authority at the Area level and to co-ordinate health services across the Area as a whole.

(1) **Role of the AHA and its Members**

2.8.   The AHA is a statutory body corporate and hence the functions described in these paragraphs relate to the Membership as a whole. The Authority has to delegate executive responsibilities to its Area Team of Officers (ATO), to individual officers at Area level, to its DMTs and to individual officers at District level, and focus the limited time of the Authority itself on the critical policy, planning and resource allocation decisions which will shape the services to be provided to the people of the Area. Thus it will review policy recommendations submitted to it by the ATO and by DMTs, and decide on Area policies and priorities within the framework of national and Regional policy. The Authority will decide guidelines on priorities and available resources so that DMTs may make realistic planning proposals. The Authority will subsequently review and challenge objectives, plans and budgets submitted to it by the ATO and the DMTs; resolve competing claims for resources between Districts; and agree a plan and budget for each District against which District performance will be assessed. The Authority will also ensure that the NHS services for which it is responsible, are planned and co-ordinated with those of the local authority.

* The types of projects to be delegated to AHAs are described in Chapter 9.

Some of its Members will therefore have places on the joint consultative committees.

2.9.   In addition, the Authority must control the performance of its officers at Area headquarters and in DMTs. To do so, it will receive reports on performance from the ATO and from each DMT, ensure that progress is according to agreed objectives, targets and budgets and that services are being provided with efficiency and economy, challenge DMTs on their performance and ensure that appropriate action is taken to correct unsatisfactory performance. The Authority will also appoint its principal officers, i.e. the officers of the ATO and DMTs and other officers who are direct appointees of the AHA. Based on its judgement of the capability of officers, the Authority will decide on the extent of delegation to them, and particularly on the extent of delegation to DMTs. To supplement these more formal methods of control, the Authority will also assess the adequacy of the services provided, through visiting by Members (subject to the functions of the FPC in relation to practice premises).

2.10.   The Authority will receive advice from its officers, but it will also consult its professional advisory machinery and receive reports from the Community Health Council (CHC). The Authority should ensure that the CHC's recommendations are acted upon by officers.

2.11.   In addition to the FPC, the AHA will need to establish other committees. These will include appointments committees, and committees (with co-opted members) for visiting and performing duties under the Mental Health Act. Except for these, the AHA should avoid establishing standing committees of Members, with or without delegated powers, to deal with particular functions (such as finance) or professions (such as nursing) or with geographic areas (such as Districts). The AHA will be a small body selected for its capability. Its Chairman will act for the Authority between meetings, consulting with the officers. Certain Members may take an interest in the affairs of particular Districts, but in so doing they will not assume executive responsibilities. The AHA will itself take all the decisions on policy, planning and resource allocation and control the performance of its officers.

(2) **Role of the DMT and its officers**

2.12.   The following paragraphs describe the functions which it will be appropriate for the AHA to delegate to DMTs.

2.13.   The members of the DMT will be responsible for managing and co-ordinating most of the operational services of the NHS. An essential part of their management task will be to formulate policies and plans for the services for which they are responsible. Thus the DMT will review the community's needs for health care and the provision of services within the District, in order to be able to assess the gaps in relation to needs. They will identify opportunities for improvements to services or changes in priorities, the aim being to provide the best possible patient care with the resources available, e.g. by shifting the balance between inpatient and domiciliary or residential care as appropriate. The DMT will discuss proposals for new or modified District policies with the ATO, either in response to new national or Regional policy guidance or in response to local

22

innovation. The DMT will subsequently develop and submit their policy proposals to the AHA.

2.14. One of the ways in which AHAs can delegate major operational responsibilities to their DMTs, while maintaining overall control and holding them accountable, will be through the planning process. DMTs will submit to the AHA, after review and discussion with the ATO and in accordance with previously agreed guidelines, comprehensive annual planning proposals recommending objectives and priorities for the development of services, allocation of resources within the District budget, allocation of additional resources to finance future projects and programmes of action, including performance targets. As part of the subsequent review and approval by AHA members, the DMT will agree targets and budgets against which both the team and individual officers will subsequently be held accountable for their performance. The DMT will then be reasonably free to manage its services within the framework of the agreed plan. Resources may subsequently be re-allocated within limits of discretion prescribed by the AHA. The DMT will report on its performance to the AHA in relation to the agreed plan.

2.15. Members of the DMT will be responsible jointly to the AHA for the functions delegated to them. The team will have right of access to the AHA and to attend any AHA meetings relevant to its own business. It will present its own plans after review and discussion with the ATO and will report on and answer for its own performance. The team will normally be represented on these occasions by a spokesman or spokesmen.

2.16. In addition to their roles as members of the DMT, the principal District officers will be accountable individually to the AHA for the management of some District services. These responsibilities are described in the section on organisational arrangements and in Part II.

2.17. In AHA(T)s, DMTs will need to co-ordinate their activities with the medical and dental schools to ensure that the appropriate balance is maintained between the service needs of the District and the needs of clinical teaching and research.

(3) Role of the Area Team of Officers

2.18. To be able to delegate executive responsibilities to DMTs, while maintaining control of performance and co-ordination between Districts, the AHA will require advice and support from an Area Team of Officers (ATO) at headquarters. The officers of the team will recommend Area-wide policies to the AHA and advise on its review of District policy proposals. The team will advise the AHA on planning guidelines for the DMTs based on a review of the Districts' identified needs for resources and national and Regional guidance. It will support the DMTs in the planning process. It will subsequently review District planning and budget proposals to test their consistency with established AHA policy and planning guidelines and advise the AHA on whether to challenge or approve District plans and on the final allocation of resources to Districts.

2.19. AHAs will be required to prepare plans jointly with their matching local authorities. ATOs will be responsible for drawing up plans in conjunction with

23

local authority chief officers for presentation to the joint consultative committees. Furthermore AHAs will have to submit their annual plans to RHAs for approval. ATOs will be responsible for preparing overall Area plans and resolving planning issues with the Regional Teams of Officers (RTO).

2.20. In addition the ATO will assist the AHA to control the performance of DMTs. For example, it will review performance information and do special analyses for the AHA, such as comparisons between Districts, to pick out issues on which the AHA should concentrate its attention. To carry out this function effectively the ATO will have monitoring and co-ordinating authority in relation to DMTs. This means that it will review and discuss District plans before their submission by the DMTs to the AHA. It will also measure, assess and report on District performance, and advise the AHA on corrective action.

2.21. The officers of the ATO will not be the managers of their District counterparts, nor will they be accountable for District performance, both sets of officers being directly accountable to the AHA. The status of officers of the ATO will however be higher than that of officers of the DMT, the difference in general increasing with the number of Districts and the size of the Area. An important aspect of the ATO's work will be to see that policies and plans agreed with the matching local authority, through the joint consultative committees, are implemented by DMTs. It will normally do this by using its monitoring and co-ordinating authority. Insofar as Area officers are accountable to the matching local education authority for the school health service, they will be able to direct the work of those officers in the Districts to whom they may assign some of their responsibilities.

2.22. In addition to their roles as members of the ATO the principal Area officers will be individually accountable for the management of some Area services. These responsibilities are described in the next section and in Part II.

2.23. In Areas not divided into Districts the functions described for the DMT and the ATO will be carried out by an Area Management Team (AMT), which, like a DMT, will include representative clinicians. The functions which will be performed by the AMT, in addition to those specified for the DMT, will be developing collaborative plans between the AHA and the local authority for consideration by the joint consultative committees, preparing the AHA's planning submission to the RHA and working on planning issues with the RTO on behalf of the AHA.

B. FUNCTIONS OF THE REGIONAL HEALTH AUTHORITY

2.24. The line of accountability will run between the statutory Authorities, i.e. AHA to RHA. The RHAs will act as the link between the AHAs and the Secretary of State and the DHSS. The RHA will be responsible for establishing priorities between the competing claims of AHAs and allocating resources to them in accordance with national guidance on policy. Thus the RHA will decide the development of medical specialities, the deployment of medical manpower and the order of major building projects. As part of its planning role, the RHA will establish guidelines on Regional policies and priorities to help its AHAs submit realistic plans and claims on RHA resources. It will also review, challenge and approve AHA plans, and subsequently control AHA performance in relation to the agreed plans.

2.25. In addition to its planning and monitoring functions, the RHA will be responsible for managing the design and construction of major capital building projects and for delegating other projects to AHAs. It will also provide some operational services from a Regional base (such as the blood transfusion service and, for Areas included in metropolitan counties, the ambulance service*), and support AHAs with the more highly specialised management services (such as operational research and computing). The RHA will employ Regional staff and also the consultants and senior registrars of non-teaching AHAs, and will be responsible for co-ordinating facilities in support of medical and dental teaching carried out by the Universities and of associated research. Except for the Chairman of the AHA, who will be appointed by the Secretary of State, and AHA Members appointed by the local authority and by Universities with medical and/or dental schools, the RHA will appoint AHA Members.

2.26 The following paragraphs describe the proposed distribution of functions between the Members and their officers. The RHA is a statutory body corporate hence the functions described below relate to the Membership as a whole.

(1) Role of the RHA and its members

2.27. The RHA has to delegate major executive responsibilities to its AHAs and to its Regional officers (for Regionally-deployed services), and focus the limited time of its Members on the important issues of policy, planning and resource allocation. The Authority can, therefore, be expected to review proposals on policies and priorities submitted to it by AHAs and by the RTO and decide on Regional policies and priorities within the framework of national policy. The Authority will establish planning guidelines for AHAs on priorities and available resources. Subsequently, it will review objectives, plans and budgets submitted to it annually by AHAs and by the RTO (for Regional services), resolve competing claims for resources between AHAs and agree targets with AHAs against which their performance can be assessed. In making planning decisions the Authority will call upon the advice of the Regional advisory committees.

2.28. In addition the RHA must control the performance of its AHAs and its Regional officers. To do so it will receive reports on AHA performance from each AHA, ensure that progress is according to plan and that services are being provided throughout the Region with efficiency and economy, challenge the performance of AHAs if necessary and ensure that appropriate remedial action is taken. It will also receive performance reports on Regionally-deployed services from its principal Regional officers. RHA Members, and the RHA Chairman in particular, will be expected to meet individual AHA Chairmen regularly to discuss the problems and opportunities of their Areas. The Authority will be responsible for appointing AHA Members, with the exceptions noted in

* In London it is proposed that one of the four metropolitan RHAs should undertake the management of the ambulance service for Greater London, through a London Ambulance Committee which will include representatives of the other three RHAs in its membership.

paragraph 2.25, and for appointing consultants and senior medical staff, with the exception of those employed by AHA(T)s.

2.29. A further important responsibility of the RHA will be to assist the Secretary of State to establish realistic national policies and priorities by providing him with information and advice on developments in the field. Thus RHA Chairmen will be expected to meet regularly with the Secretary of State and with senior officers of the DHSS.

(2) Role of the Regional Team of Officers

2.30. If the RHA is to delegate major responsibilities to AHAs while maintaining ultimate control of AHA performance, it must have strong advice and support from its Regional staff. The Regional Team of Officers (RTO) will therefore be responsible for recommending Regional policies to the RHA and advising on its approval of AHA policies. The RTO will prepare a Regional development plan, including the distribution of medical specialties, deployment of medical manpower and the scheduling of major capital projects, for decision and approval by the RHA. It will recommend to the RHA planning guidelines on priorities and available resources for AHAs based on a review of Areas' identified needs for resources, and national planning guidance. The RTO will subsequently review AHA planning and budget proposals to test their consistency with established RHA policy and planning guidelines and advise the RHA on whether to challenge or approve AHA plans and on the final allocation of resources. In addition it will prepare the RHA's planning submission to the Secretary of State and work on planning issues with the Regional divisions of the DHSS. Regional officers will keep in close contact with their professional counterparts in the DHSS, and in so doing they will help contribute towards the formulation of realistic national policies.

2.31. The RTO will also assist the RHA control the performance of AHAs. Thus the RTO will review information on AHA performance and perform special analyses for the RHA (such as comparisons between AHAs), in order to pick out the important issues on which the RHA should concentrate its attention. The RTO will have monitoring and co-ordinating authority to ATOs, but RTO members will not be the managers of their counterparts in the Areas. The RTO will review and discuss AHA plans before their submission by the AHAs to the RHA, will measure, assess and report on AHA performance and advise the RHA on corrective action to be taken by AHAs.

2.32. In addition to their roles as members of the RTO, the principal Regional officers will be accountable individually for the management of certain Regional services. These responsibilities are described in Section II of this Chapter and in Part II.

C. FUNCTIONS OF THE SECRETARY OF STATE

2.33. The Secretary of State with the DHSS will be responsible for establishing national policies and priorities which will determine the kind, scale and balance of services to be provided by the NHS. They will agree with RHAs, in the light of national objectives, appropriate long-term objectives, priorities and target standards of care, as guidelines for subsequent Regional and Area planning. Subsequently, they will review and approve RHA plans, and allocate resources between the competing claims of RHAs. The family practitioner services will be funded by the DHSS outside Regional and Area budgets.

2.34.   The Secretary of State will be accountable for the performance of the NHS and must maintain control of the performance of functions delegated to RHAs. The DHSS will therefore monitor Regional performance in relation to agreed objectives, and targets including controlling revenue and capital income and expenditure. The Secretary of State will appoint RHA Members and the Chairmen of AHAs. RHAs will be accountable to him and the Secretary of State will have powers of direction over them. In addition the DHSS will obtain, develop or control certain resources which influence the adequacy, efficiency and economy of the Service (e.g. remuneration and conditions of service, number and distribution of certain staff, and transactions, major building projects etc.), and give certain centralised supporting services which can be provided more economically on a national basis (e.g. some types of research, supplies, etc.).

2.35.   The organisation and operation of the DHSS are to be overhauled in order to enable it to fill this role in the reorganised NHS (see Appendix 2). The total organisation structure of the reorganised NHS is shown in Exhibit III.

Section II—Organisation at Each Level

2.36.   This section gives a general description of the organisation at each level —District, Area and Region. Fuller descriptions of the organisation within each skill group are given in Part II of the report. An important feature of the organisation at each level is the multi-disciplinary team introduced in Chapter I. The joint responsibilities of the team described in the preceding section are to be distinguished from the responsibilities which members of the team have individually. The individual responsibilities of the team members at each level are outlined in this section and more fully described in Part II and in the role specifications in Appendix 3.

2.37.   It is particularly necessary to define individual responsibilities of team members in relation to planning, not only because planning is an important part of the management task at each level, but also because planning is largely a team activity. The individual responsibilities will vary according to the subject matter of the planning activity and the stage in the planning process.

a. The subject matter of planning activities will be of two kinds, the *operational health-care services*, such as geriatric services, primary and preventive-care services, accident and emergency services etc., and *other operational and supporting services*, such as laundry, catering and personnel services. Planning for the first kind of services will often affect the second kind. But the second kind can sometimes be planned independently of the first.
b. There are three main stages in planning: "*formulation*", when needs are identified, objectives set and a plan drawn up to achieve the objectives;

27

EXHIBIT III

FRAMEWORK OF THE ORGANISATION STRUCTURE

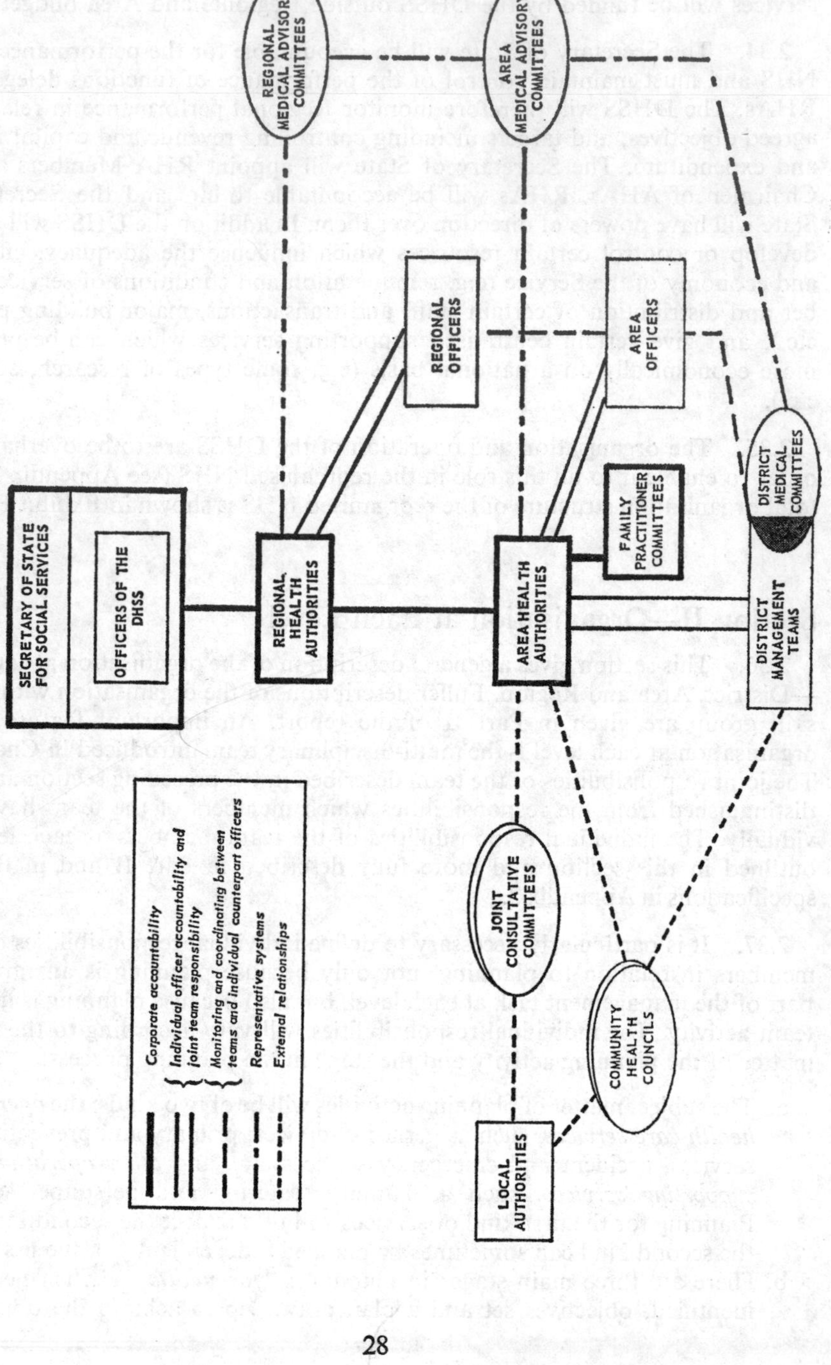

REGIONAL MEDICAL ADVISORY COMMITTEES

AREA MEDICAL ADVISORY COMMITTEES

SECRETARY OF STATE FOR SOCIAL SERVICES

OFFICERS OF THE DHSS

REGIONAL OFFICERS

REGIONAL HEALTH AUTHORITIES

AREA OFFICERS

AREA HEALTH AUTHORITIES

FAMILY PRACTITIONER COMMITTEES

DISTRICT MEDICAL COMMITTEES

DISTRICT MANAGEMENT TEAMS

JOINT CONSULTATIVE COMMITTEES

COMMUNITY HEALTH COUNCILS

LOCAL AUTHORITIES

Corporate accountability

Individual officer accountability and joint team responsibility

Monitoring and coordinating between teams and individual counterpart officers

Representative systems

External relationships

"*approval*", when the plan is adopted by those empowered to take this decision; and "*implication*", when a programme for implementation is drawn up and responsibilities for implementation assigned to individuals.

The individual responsibilities in planning as set out in this section reflect these different kinds of subject matter and stages of planning.

2.38. In the *formulative* stage of plans for *operational health-care services* the specialist in community medicine will take the lead and co-ordinate the activity. Other members of the team will formulate plans for deployment of resources, particularly manpower, for which each is responsible in relation to the plan for operational health-care services (e.g. the nursing officer will prepare the nursing plans and the administrator the other operational and support services plans). In the *formulative* stage of plans, for operational and supporting services not immediately linked to an operational health-care service plan, the administrator will be the co-ordinator. He will also be responsible for co-ordinating the total planning process by assisting the team to prepare a comprehensive planning proposal for the *approval* stage. During the *implementation* stage the administrator will ensure that the team has a complete programme of implementation so that each member of the team can carry out his individual responsibilities in implementing plans.

A. DISTRICT ORGANISATION

2.39. The proposed District organisation has four main features:

(1) A District Management Team (DMT) to effect integration at District level through planning and co-ordination.
(2) Health-care planning teams to plan services which contribute towards groups of needs.
(3) Integration within the skill groups which provide patient care and supporting services.
. (4) Co-ordination below District level.

(1) The District Management Team

2.40. The functions of the DMT are set out in Section I (paragraphs 2.13 and 2.14). Its composition is designed to integrate the total range of services at the District level—one of the key features introduced in Chapter 1. It also enables consultants and general practitioners to participate directly in the management process—another of the key features.

2.41. The DMT will therefore consist of:

Two elected medical representatives, one a consultant, the other a general practitioner
District Community Physician
District Nursing Officer
District Finance Officer
District Administrator

Certain other officers at District level, not being members of the DMT, will have the right to attend team meetings and participate in discussions affecting their services (see paragraph 1.26 of Chapter 1). Furthermore, in Districts of an AHA (T) where undergraduate medical and/or dental teaching is being carried out, representatives of the teaching school (who might be the deans) will attend team meetings in order that the operational policies of the District and plans for the development of District services may take account of the needs of clinical teaching and research.

2.42. The DMT will be a group of equals, no member being the managerial superior of another. The team thus brings together, to make decisions and to share in joint responsibility, both clinicians and officers accountable to the AHA for hierarchically-organised services. It will be the responsibility of each member of the team to ensure that inter-disciplinary issues are resolved within the team. In resolving such issues the team will act as a consensus-forming group, i.e. no decisions can be taken that override the opposition of a team member. An issue remaining unresolved will pass for resolution to the AHA.

2.43. The frequency of meetings of the DMT will depend on the extent to which it conducts its business through formal team meetings. In general the team may be expected to meet no more frequently than once a week and no less frequently than once a month.

2.44. "Joint responsibility" (see paragraph 2.42) means that the AHA will expect the members of the DMT to co-operate in order to reach a consensus view and to be bound by team decisions. The officers of the ATO will monitor their counterpart officers in order to ensure that they contribute effectively to the work of the DMT. If the work of the DMT is found unacceptable by the AHA, the DMT will not be held corporately accountable, but the AHA, with the assistance of the Area officers, will assess the performance of each team member to determine the source of the difficulty.

2.45. The Chairman (see paragraph 1.27) of the DMT will have the specific functions of:

a. Chairing the formal meetings of the team, deciding its agenda for such meetings, and being generally responsible for the conduct and the follow-through of meetings. When a member other than the administrator is Chairman, he will, having regard to the administrator's responsibilities for general co-ordination, act in conjunction with the administrator in respect of the latter functions.
b. Acting as spokesman for the DMT in presenting service-planning proposals to the AHA, in conjunction with such other member or members of the DMT as may be appropriate.

More generally the Chairman will have the task of helping the team to agree on crucial issues, not only in formal meetings, but by discussion between the meetings with individual members, and will, where necessary, seek to stimulate ideas and action over the whole field of the team's joint responsibilities.

(2) Health-care planning teams

2.46. The DMT will be responsible for identifying gaps in its services in relation to needs and for developing ways of improving its services to use

30

existing resources better. For example, it will examine ways of changing existing patterns of care, by alterations in operational policies and procedures and in priorities between services. This team activity will relate both to the operational health-care services and to the related supporting services. In order to carry out the planning of the operational health-care services, the DMT will establish a number of multi-disciplinary health-care planning teams to concentrate on planning services to meet particular groups of needs.

2.47.   The health-care planning teams can take two forms. They can be either *permanent* teams with continuing responsibilities or *ad hoc* teams established to examine specific issues.

a. Certain groups of needs require (in the services which are provided to meet them), a high level of interaction between hospital and community care. It is these services which have most to gain from unification of the NHS. Consequently they are likely to change in the years following 1974. They will require continuous planning and monitoring. Examples are:
Elderly
Children
Maternity
Mentally ill
Mentally handicapped

It is desirable that there should be some uniformity in the scope of the teams set up on a continuing basis and hence national and Regional policies may be developed to guide DMTs in setting up their teams.

b. Other groups of needs, often resulting in demands on the acute services of the hospital, will require a different form of planning and co-ordinative effort. Special studies may have to be carried out by *ad hoc* multi-disciplinary teams, which would identify the required changes, programme and monitor their implementation, and disband on completion of the project. Examples are:
Review of primary-care services
Introduction of day surgery
Reorganisation of an outpatients' department
A review of services for people with epilepsy.

2.48.   The composition of these health-care planning teams will need to be adjusted to particular situations but there will probably have to be representation of general practitioners, consultants, hospital and community nurses, health visitors, relevant paramedical staff and representatives of local authority services, particularly social services. They will be supported by the District Community Physician and an administrator.

2.49.   The role of the health-care planning teams will be to assess needs in order to effect changes in services. This involves four kinds of activity:

a. **Continuously reviewing needs of particular groups and the services being provided to meet these needs.** The purpose will be to identify gaps in service provision and the opportunities for improvement.

31

b. **Contributing to policy recommendations and to development of the annual District plan.** The teams will advise the DMT on the policy recommendations to make to the AHA. They will, for example, examine the relevance of new national policy guidance to the local situation. They will also develop the relevant part of the annual planning proposals for the District.

c. **Carrying out special studies to establish ways of bringing about beneficial change.** They will develop plans and programmes of action to implement identified improvement opportunities. The DMT will examine their proposals and decide on priorities.

d. **Assisting the DMT to monitor and co-ordinate the implementation of projects and assess results.** All members of teams will be responsible for assisting with the proposed changes. They will do this as a service to the DMT. After implementation they will assess the effects of the change.

2.50.   Team members will take part both in the formulation of plans and in their implementation. They will bring to the planning process their own particular knowledge and skills. They will form a link with professional opinion in their own disciplines, bringing representative views to the team and advising on what is practical and acceptable. Thus the consultant on the team will be responsible for ensuring that relevant medical issues are raised and discussed at meetings of the appropriate division of the District Medical Committee. Team members will also be expected to inform their colleagues on new developments. Exhibit IV illustrates the composition and functions of some health-care teams.

2.51.   Data must be gathered and analysed if teams are to work effectively, and the teams must have administrative support to draw up reports and co-ordinate their meetings and work. The District Community Physician will be a member of each team and will contribute his knowledge of the epidemiology of the District. He will carry out special studies and analyses for the teams. Each team will be supported by an administrator who will provide a service both to the community physician and to the planning team. The teams should also be supported and advised by specialist planning staff from Area headquarters.

2.52.   Each team should have a chairman, selected from among their number by the members. His role would be to secure the good working relationships necessary for co-operation in planning.

(3) Integration of skill groups

2.53.   Through the composition of the DMT it will be possible to co-ordinate the work of the various skill groups in the Districts. A description of each skill group is included in Part II. The following paragraphs indicate some important features in the organisation of the skill groups and outline the responsibilities of individual members of the DMT. Role specifications are included in Appendix 3.

2.54.   Important new features of the organisation of the skill groups are:

a. A single District Medical Committee to represent clinicians.
b. The District Community Physician, a specialist in community medicine.

32

EXHIBIT IV

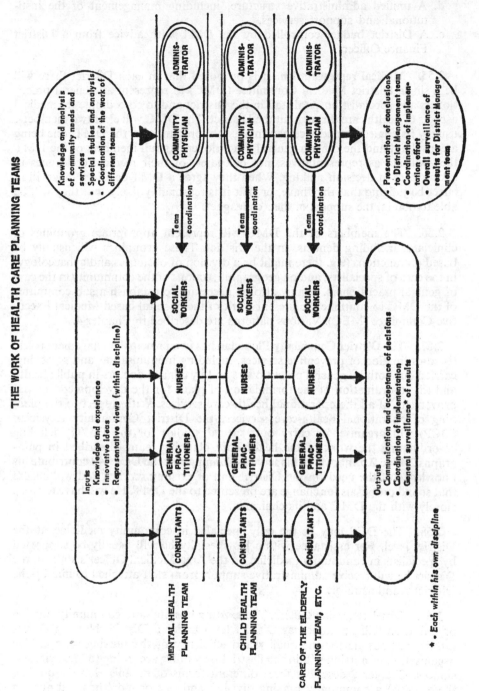

THE WORK OF HEALTH CARE PLANNING TEAMS

Inputs
- Knowledge and experience
- Innovative ideas
- Representative views (within discipline)

- Knowledge and analysis of community needs and services
- Special studies and analysis
- Coordination of the work of different teams

- Presentation of conclusions to District Management team
- Coordination of implementation effort
- Overall surveillance of results for District Management team

MENTAL HEALTH PLANNING TEAM

CHILD HEALTH PLANNING TEAM

CARE OF THE ELDERLY PLANNING TEAM, ETC.

CONSULTANTS   GENERAL PRACTITIONERS   NURSES   SOCIAL WORKERS   COMMUNITY PHYSICIAN   ADMINISTRATOR

Team coordination

Outputs
- Communication and acceptance of decisions
- Coordination of implementation
- General surveillance* of results

* - Each within his own discipline

33

c. A unified hospital and community nursing service.
d. A unified administrative structure, including management of the institutional and support services.
e. A District budget controlled by the DMT with advice from a District Finance Officer.

2.55. **Medical representation.** It is proposed that in each District there will be a single District Medical Committee (DMC) to represent all general practitioners and specialist hospital staff in the District and to co-ordinate the medical aspects of health care throughout the District. The DMC will elect two members, usually its chairman and vice chairman, to represent it on the DMT, one being a consultant and the other a general practitioner. As full members of the DMT they will act as representatives, not delegates, of their medical colleagues in taking part in decision making. When they agree a DMT decision, they will in effect be judging that they have, or that it is reasonably likely that they will be able to obtain, the support of their colleagues.

2.56. The members of the DMC will represent appropriate groupings of clinicians, including dentists, in the District. These groupings will usually be based on functions (e.g. there might be a division of obstetrics and gynaecology) in the case of specialists, and on geographic sections of the community in the case of general practitioners. It may also be necessary to establish a sub-committee of the DMC to continue the present work of the hospital based Medical Executive Committee (MEC). Various patterns are described in Chapter 4.

2.57. **The District Community Physician** has two principal management roles: (i) co-ordination of preventive services, including immunisation and screening, carried out both by general practitioners and by clinical doctors in public health and (ii) co-ordination of the formulation of plans for the development, or improvement, of all the operational health-care services. With respect to the planning of operational health-care services, the District Community Physician (DCP) will organise, or carry out, special studies for the DMT, including co-ordinating the work of the health-care planning teams described in paragraphs 2.47 to 2.52 above. In his service-planning role the DCP will contribute his knowledge of the needs in the District and of existing services and will ensure that sound proposals for change are presented to the DMT. He will have to work closely with the DMC and its chairman.

2.58. The DCP may be the only specialist in community medicine at the District level. For assistance within his specialty he will usually be supported by specialists in community medicine on the Area Medical Officer's staff. In the District he will receive administrative support from staff attached to him by the District Administrator.

2.59. **District Nursing Officer.** The existing hospital and community nursing organisation will be unified at District level under a District Nursing Officer (DNO) responsible for the quality and efficiency of the nursing service. The organisation of nursing within the District may differ according to local circumstances. Chapter 8 describes three different forms of organisation. In outline, these are (i) a community nursing division and one or more hospital nursing divisions, with separate heads of the community and hospital nursing services accountable to the DNO; (ii) a number of functional divisions, together with a primary-care division, with divisional heads accountable to the DNO. There would be attachment of nurses to general practitioners and co-ordination, at an appropriate level, on a geographic basis with social work teams; (iii) functional divisions only (e.g. geriatrics or midwifery), including both the relevant hospital and community nurses.

2.60. The DNO will be responsible for preparing a plan for the nursing services in the District, for ensuring that priorities are established in connection with demands upon nursing resources from the various planning teams, for managing nursing services and for co-ordinating any necessary changes in nursing organisation consequent upon implementation of agreed plans.

2.61. **District Finance Officer.** The DMT will prepare a budget within AHA policies and planning guidelines for the AHA's approval. The District Finance Officer (DFO) will be responsible for providing the DMT with the necessary financial services, information, guidance and advice. All officers of the DMT will have their own budgetary responsibilities and the DFO will provide them with the necessary financial reports and analyses. He will have a special, but not exclusive, responsibility for seeing that services are provided economically and efficiently.

2.62. With respect to planning, the DFO will translate planning proposals into financial terms, will interpret these to his DMT colleagues and to the members of the planning teams, and will co-ordinate the budgetary aspects of the DMT's planning process.

2.63. **District Administrator.** The District Administrator (DA) will have three principal management roles; (i) general administrative co-ordination for the DMT and within the District; (ii) the management of administrative services; and (iii) the management of institutional and support services.

2.64. As part of his function of general administrative co-ordination, the DA will be responsible for the co-ordination of the total planning process. Thus, for example, he will ensure that comprehensive District planning proposals are drawn up for presentation to the AHA and its ATO. He will need to see that the various aspects of the planning process, for which team members have individual co-ordinating responsibility, are co-ordinated with each other within a total programme. He will himself be responsible for the formulation of plans for all support services, and will be accountable for co-ordinating the implementation of agreed plans.

2.65. The DA's management of administrative services will include the provision of support to other officers and teams as regards such matters as secretariat, personnel and planning services, management services and relations with the public and press. His responsibilities for institutional and operational services will include the management of hotel services (catering, domestic, portering), laundry, CSSD and transport services, and the administration of institutions and co-ordination of services below District level. The detailed pattern of organisation will depend on the characteristics of the District, especially on the situation and kinds of institutions. Alternatives are given in Chapter 11.

2.66. **Paramedical and other services.** It will be desirable to organise the diagnostic and therapeutic services so as to provide a service to medical practitioners and their patients throughout the District. Organisational arrangements for the management of pharmaceutical services are described in Chapter 6 and of paramedical services in Chapter 7.

Co-ordination below District level.

2.67. In each skill group there will be management levels below the level of District management and there will be a corresponding need for the co-ordination of activities, e.g. medical, nursing, paramedical and various institutional services such as catering, domestic work and portering, below that level.

2.68. The administrative organisation will include administrators ("sector administrators") responsible for managing or co-ordinating the institutional and support services within single large institutions or within groups of institutions in sectors of the District. It will be advantageous if the main skill groups (particularly nursing and administration) are so organised that there can be liaison at appropriate levels. Such liaison may be informal or there may be multidisciplinary teams established within institutions or sectors. The framework of the District organisation is illustrated in Exhibit V.

B. AREA ORGANISATION

2.69. The Area organisation has been designed to carry out the functions described in Section I of this Chapter, that is, to support the AHA in joint planning with the matching local authorities, to assist Districts with their planning to review their proposals, and to monitor and evaluate District performance. In addition Area officers will have executive functions in relation to services deployed from an Area base. The following paragraphs accordingly describe the roles of:

(1) The Area Team of Officers.
(2) Area officers in the functions for which they will be individually accountable.

Area Team of Officers

2.70. It is proposed that the Area Team of Officers shall consist of:

> Area Medical Officer.
> Area Nursing Officer.
> Area Treasurer.
> Area Administrator.

2.71. The Area Team of Officers (ATO), unlike the DMT, will not include elected clinical representatives.* There will be other Area officers directly

---

* This section describes the team of officers in an Area with DMTs. In an Area without Districts the team will include two representatives of an Area Medical Committee and the team will be known as the "Area Management Team" (see para 2.23).

EXHIBIT V

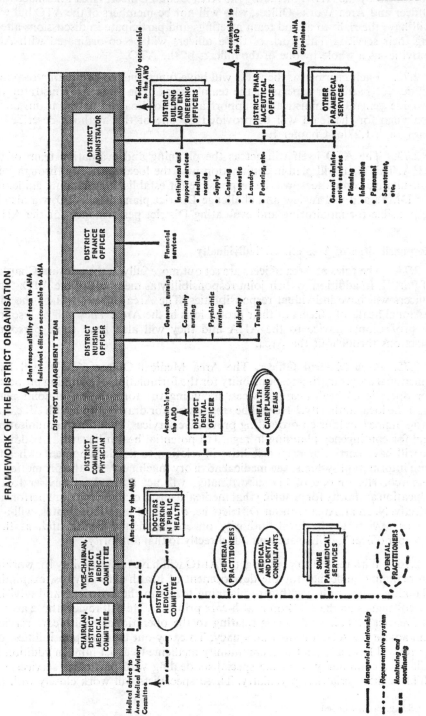

FRAMEWORK OF THE DISTRICT ORGANISATION

appointed by the AHA, including the Area Dental Officer, Area Pharmaceutical Officer and Area Works Officer, who will not be members of the ATO but who will have the right to attend team meetings and participate in discussions affecting their services. The work of these officers will be co-ordinated with Area activities as a whole by one of the officers of the ATO.

2.72. Each member of the ATO will have functional co-ordinating responsibilities for particular aspects of the team's work. The Area Administrator will provide general administrative support and co-ordination to the team, and a chairman for the team will be provided by one of the methods described in paragraph 1.27 of Chapter 1.

2.73. The ATO itself will act as the planning and evaluation team of the AHA. This team will plan in conjunction with the local authority through joint consultative committees, will be responsible for establishing planning guidelines for DMTs and will review and challenge District plans. The ATO will also be responsible for monitoring and evaluating District performance for the AHA.

Responsibilities of Area officers individually

2.74. The roles of Area officers are set out more fully in the relevant Chapters of Part II. In addition to their joint responsibility as members of the ATO, these officers will have individual responsibilities. The Area officers will be the professional heads of officers of their professions in the Area. They will be a source of professional advice to the AHA and they will also have some personnel functions throughout the Area.

2.75. **Area Medical Officer.** The Area Medical Officer (AMO) will have functional co-ordinating responsibility for the formulation of planning proposals for operational health-care services, including the formulation of joint plans with the local authority.* He will be responsible for drawing up health education programmes and for co-ordinating preventive services, including immunisation, and for contingency planning in regard to potential health hazards. In addition he will have particular responsibilities in relation to the development of health-care information systems, the medical advisory machinery and the promotion of research. He, or one of his subordinates, will act as medical adviser to the education authority for ensuring that medical aspects of the service are performed effectively. In an Area without Districts he, or one of his subordinates, will also act as adviser to the local authority on environmental health and, as their "proper officer", will be accountable directly to that authority.

2.76. With respect to planning, the AMO will have responsibility for working up planning guidelines for the development of health-care services, examining planning issues with health-care planning teams in the Districts, and advising his colleagues on the ATO on health-care priorities. He will review those aspects of District planning proposals relating to the operational health-care services and advise the ATO on their adequacy. To carry out these responsibilities, the AMO will have a specialist in community medicine to assist him. In addition he will have community medicine specialists dealing with particular services, e.g. child health, geriatrics, psychiatry. These specialists will work closely with the

* See para 2.37 et seq.

matching local authority on joint planning issues and will advise the AMO, DCPs and health-care planning teams in the Districts.

2.77. **Area Nursing Officer.** The Area Nursing Officer (ANO) will contribute her nursing skills to the planning and evaluation process of the ATO. The ANO will also work closely with the AMO in joint planning with the local authority. She will be responsible to the local authority for providing nursing advice and services in matters which are its statutory responsibility. She will also be responsible, through a subordinate, for co-ordinating the nursing aspects of the school health service, for which some responsibilities may be assigned to DNOs.

2.78. **Area Treasurer.** The Area Treasurer (AT) will be responsible for providing advice on all financial matters to the AHA and its officers; for co-ordinating preparation of the financial estimates; for preparing the statutory accounts; for providing accountancy and cashier services; for control systems and financial information to management; for monitoring the use of resources and for providing financial supervision and internal audit.

2.79. **Area Administrator.** There will be two aspects to the role of the Area Administrator (AA): (i) providing general administrative co-ordination for the ATO and acting as Secretary to the AHA and (ii) managing or co-ordinating some Area-deployed services.

2.80. As part of his general administrative function, the AA will have general co-ordinating responsibilities for the planning process throughout the Area as a whole. This will mean that he will co-ordinate the work of the ATO in establishing guidelines for DMTs. He will also co-ordinate the review of District plans and the final preparation of the AHA's formal planning submission to the RHA. Each member of the ATO will have specific individual responsibilities in relation to preparing guidelines and drawing up and reviewing plans for their own services. It will be the role of the AA to help the team ensure that the total planning activity progresses within an agreed programme. The AA will also give planning advice and assistance to the planning activities in the Districts, both by DMTs and by health-care planning teams.

2.81. He will also be responsible for providing support to other officers of the team in their personnel and planning functions, and will assist with management services. These services will be provided through subordinate administrators on his staff. The administrator to serve the FPC will be provided from the AA's staff. Depending on the characteristics of the Area, the AA will manage directly a number of services, including ambulances, supplies, central laundries and CSSDs etc. He will co-ordinate the function of the Area Works Officer, who will be responsible for carrying out capital building projects delegated to the Area, for the provision of specialist maintenance services and for monitoring and co-ordinating maintenance at District level.

*　　　*　　　*

The framework of an AHA organisation with Districts is illustrated in Exhibit VI, and that of an AHA not divided into Districts in Exhibit VII.

C. REGIONAL ORGANISATION

2.82. The regional organisation has been designed to carry out the functions described in Section I of this Chapter. This section describes the proposed

EXHIBIT VI

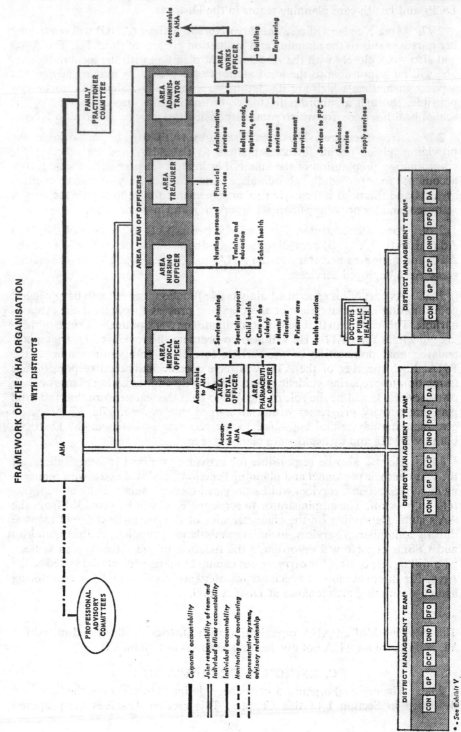

FRAMEWORK OF THE AHA ORGANISATION
WITH DISTRICTS

EXHIBIT VII

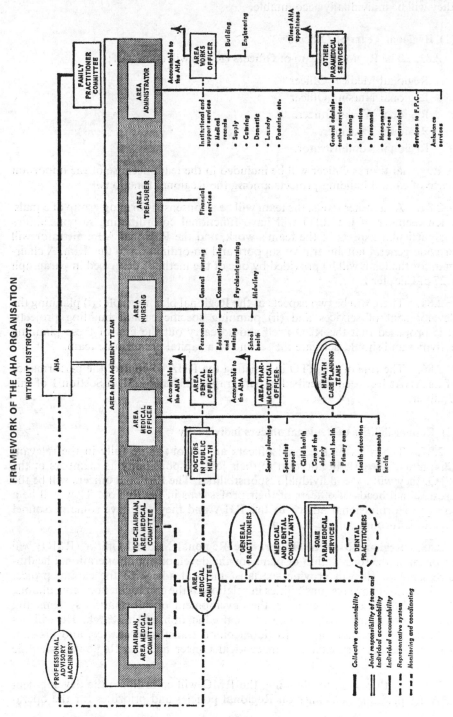

FRAMEWORK OF THE AHA ORGANISATION
WITHOUT DISTRICTS

Regional Team of Officers, and also sets out the various functions for which they will be individually accountable.

(1) Regional Team of Officers

2.83.   The Regional Team of Officers (RTO) will consist of:

Regional Medical Officer
Regional Nursing Officer
Regional Works Officer.
Regional Treasurer.
Regional Administrator.

A Regional Works Officer will be included in the team because of the important place of capital building projects among the Regional functions.

2.84.   As at other levels, the team will be a consensus-forming group of equals. Each member of the RTO will have functional co-ordinating responsibilities for particular aspects of the team's work, and the Regional Administrator will provide general administrative support and co-ordination to the team. A chairman for the team will be provided by one of the methods described in paragraph 1.27 of Chapter 1.

2.85.   There will be two aspects of the Regional planning role: (i) planning the development of services and (ii) planning specific capital building projects. It is proposed that the RTO itself should carry out the first of these planning activities and should delegate the second to a capital programme team.

2.86.   The role of the RTO in assisting the RHA to control the performance of its AHAs has been described in paragraphs 2.30 and 2.31 in Section 1 of this Chapter.

(2) Responsibilities of Regional officers individually

2.87.   The roles of Regional officers are set out more fully in the relevant Chapters of Part II. In addition to their joint responsibility as members of the RTO, they will have individual responsibilities. The Regional officers will be the professional heads of officers of their professions in the Region. They will be a source of professional advice to the RHA and they will have some personnel functions throughout the Region.

2.88.   **Regional Medical Officer.** The Regional Medical Officer (RMO) will co-ordinate the formulation of plans for the development of operational health-care services. He will provide specialist medical advice to the capital project team, and will have responsibilities in relation to the employment of consultants, the medical advisory machinery, the development of information systems and undergraduate and postgraduate medical education and research. He will co-ordinate the direction of the Regional blood transfusion service, and his staff will include the Regional Pharmaceutical Officer and the Regional Scientific Officer.

2.89.   With respect to planning, the RMO will co-ordinate the development of AHA planning guidelines on Regional policies and priorities for the operational health-care services, including priorities for the distribution of medical specialties, the deployment of medical manpower and the scheduling of starts of capital building projects. He will also be responsible for reviewing AHA planning proposals for operational health-care services, with particular reference to the agreed guidelines. These Regional planning activities will usually be carried out as a team activity by the RTO. However, multi-disciplinary service-planning teams may be established to support the RTO. The RMO will be responsible for co-ordinating the work of these teams. He will be assisted in this function by a subordinate specialist in community medicine. Other subordinates will, in addition to their functional responsibilities, specialise in particular subjects, e.g. psychiatry. These medical officers will advise the RMO and will take part in the service-planning teams.

2.90. **Regional Nursing Officer.** The Regional Nursing Officer (RNO) will be responsible for providing advice on nursing matters to the RHA, will contribute her nursing skills to the planning and evaluation process and will give specialist nursing advice to project teams for capital works.

2.91. **Regional Works Officer.** The Regional Works Officer (RWO) will be accountable for the co-ordination of the Regional architectural, engineering, and quantity surveying services, for the design and construction of new buildings and building and engineering maintenance for the Region.

2.92. **Regional Treasurer.** The Regional Treasurer (RT) will co-ordinate the preparation of budgets for the team as part of the overall planning process and will give both the RHA and the team financial advice, including performing any detailed special financial analyses. He will also be responsible for co-ordinating financial practice and systems throughout the Region. He will monitor the performance of AHAs generally for economy and efficiency in the use of resources.

2.93. **Regional Administrator.** There will be two aspects to the work of the Regional Administrator (RA): (i) providing general administrative co-ordination as a service to the RTO and acting as Secretary to the RHA and (ii) managing some services deployed from a Regional base. He will, for example, manage Regionally-based ambulance services and will be accountable for the administrative aspects of the capital building programme. He will provide personnel and management services to other members of the RTO and to the Region as a whole.

2.94. With respect to planning, the RA will have general co-ordinating responsibilities for the development, support and maintenance of the planning process throughout the Region as a whole. He will ensure that AHAs submit their plans to the RHA in the approved manner and within planning deadlines. In doing so, he may have to provide skilled planning assistance to AHAs to support them in their planning activity. In relation to the RTO, the RA will co-ordinate the process of formulating a comprehensive set of AHA planning guidelines to recommend to the RHA. He will also co-ordinate the subsequent review of AHA planning proposals and the preparation of the RHA's planning submission to the DHSS. Within this process, each member of the RTO will have specific planning responsibilities. It will be the role of the Administrator therefore, in addition to his own planning responsibilities, to help the team

43

by co-ordinating the total planning activity in relation to its agreed programme. He will have on his staff planning experts, such as statisticians, who will work with medical officers and others to assist them in their planning responsibilities.

2.95.　Either the RA or the RMO will be responsible for the co-ordination and administrative control of the capital building programme, with the support of a multi-disciplinary team. Whichever is responsible, he will also be responsible for co-ordinating the preparation of briefs for individual capital projects, supported by multi-disciplinary project teams.

*　　*　　*

The framework of an RHA organisation is illustrated in Exhibit VIII

2.96.　This concludes the summary description in this Chapter of the internal organisation of RHAs and AHAs and of the relations between them and with the DHSS. There follows, in Chapter 3, an outline of some important processes to be used within these organisations.

CHAPTER 3
MANAGEMENT PROCESSES

3.1.　This Chapter describes some of the main management processes that must accompany the new management structure, in particular planning, monitoring and control, and personnel management. As explained in Chapter 1 the planning process, combined with selective monitoring and control, is the means by which decentralisation of decision making will be combined with central strategic direction and control.

Section I—Planning

3.2.　Chapter 2 describes how the new Authorities will be organised, and the part that each management level and its senior officers should play individually in the planning process. This section draws these strands together and describes the new planning process as a whole, in two subsections describing the planning cycle and responsibilities for planning work, and the preparation of plans for each District.

A. THE PLANNING CYCLE

3.3.　All levels in the reorganised NHS have a part to play at all times in the planning process.

　　a. AHAs will set policies and standards for their Areas as a whole, allocate resources to Districts, plan services to be provided in Districts, plan directly certain Area-level services and collaborate with local authorities in planning.

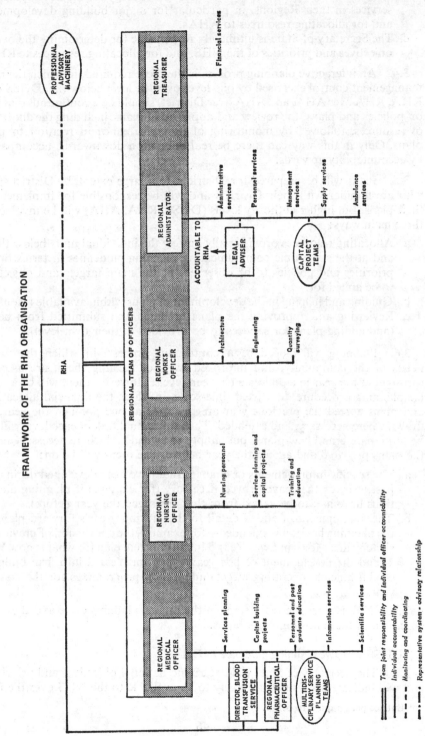

EXHIBIT VIII

FRAMEWORK OF THE RHA ORGANISATION

RHA

PROFESSIONAL ADVISORY MACHINERY

REGIONAL TEAM OF OFFICERS

REGIONAL MEDICAL OFFICER
- Services planning
- Capital building projects
- Personnel and post graduate education
- Information services
- Scientific services

DIRECTOR, BLOOD TRANSFUSION SERVICE

REGIONAL PHARMACEUTICAL OFFICER

MULTIDISCIPLINARY SERVICE PLANNING TEAMS

REGIONAL NURSING OFFICER
- Nursing personnel
- Service planning and capital projects
- Training and education

REGIONAL WORKS OFFICER
- Architecture
- Engineering
- Quantity surveying

ACCOUNTABLE TO RHA

LEGAL ADVISER

CAPITAL PROJECT TEAMS

REGIONAL ADMINISTRATOR
- Administrative services
- Personnel services
- Management services
- Supply services
- Ambulance services

REGIONAL TREASURER
- Financial services

Team joint responsibility and individual officer accountability

Individual accountability

Monitoring and coordinating

Representative system - advisory relationship

45

b. RHAs will be responsible for developing a strategy for the development of services in their Regions, in particular for major building developments, and for allocating resources to AHAs.

c. The Secretary of State is ultimately responsible for determining the overall objectives and priorities of the NHS, and for allocating resources to RHAs.

3.4. An interactive planning process is therefore required, in which the main management control exercised by one level over the level below (i.e. DHSS over RHA, RHA over AHA, and AHA over District) should be a continuous dialogue on policies and plans, the review and approval of plans, including the allocation of resources, followed by monitoring of its performance in relation to these plans. Only in this way can there be real delegation downwards, accompanied by accountability upwards.

3.5. Plans will be prepared for Districts, to a large extent, by District staff* who are familiar with their Districts and will be responsible for implementing their plans. But higher authority levels (DHSS, RHA, AHA) will be involved in three main ways:

a. Allocating resources provisionally among the individual units below them, and at the same time communicating planning guidelines in terms of the priorities and policies to be observed, or the main targets and objectives to be aimed for.

b. Guiding and helping in the development of plans within available resources.

c. Reviewing and approving the plans prepared and submitted from below (and adding plans for services to be provided at their own level).

3.6. Planning will indeed be a continuous process, in which the future needs of the community, and improved ways of meeting them, are assessed throughout the year in a dialogue between levels. However, there will be a regular planning procedure, to a fixed time-scale, in which the financial allocations and plans agreed the previous year are reviewed at one point in the year, redrawn where necessary, and extended. Thus the annual task at each level will not be to prepare brand new plans, but simply to extend and where necessary revise the plans prepared and agreed the year before. The focus will be on:

a. The specific improvements or changes that have been developed during the past year, or that have proved necessary (for example if planning allocations have had to be varied from that envisaged the year before).

b. The development of added detail to the previous year's forward plans as the planning horizon is extended—for example, the conversion of previously sketchy ideas for what was Year 5 into a concrete plan for what is now Year 4, and the development of last year's plan for Year 2 into firm budgets, establishments, operating targets and action programmes for the coming year.

Exhibit IX illustrates the main steps in the annual planning cycle and these are described in the following paragraphs.

(1) DHSS will give planning guidance to RHAs

3.7. The Secretary of State will determine national objectives and priorities, and will indicate what sums are likely to be available to the NHS over the next

_____
* But see paragraph 3.16 below.

EXHIBIT IX

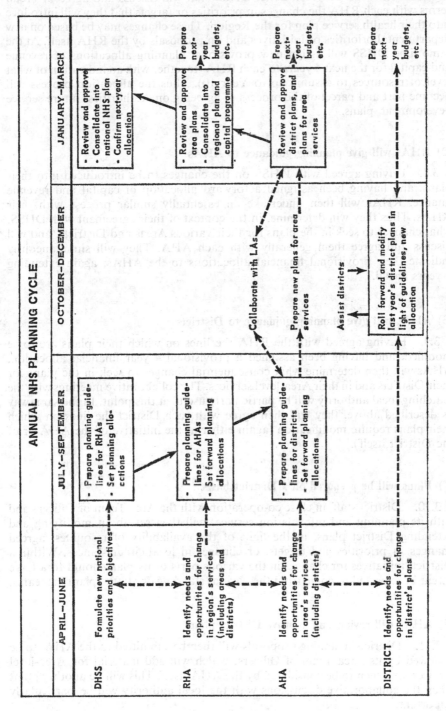

ANNUAL NHS PLANNING CYCLE

	APRIL—JUNE	JULY—SEPTEMBER	OCTOBER—DECEMBER	JANUARY—MARCH
DHSS	Formulate new national priorities and objectives	- Prepare planning guidelines for RHAs - Set planning allocations		- Review and approve - Consolidate into national NHS plan - Confirm next-year allocation
RHA	Identify needs and opportunities for change in region's services (including areas and districts)	- Prepare planning guidelines for AHAs - Set forward planning allocations		- Review and approve area plans - Consolidate into regional plan and capital programme
AHA	Identify needs and opportunities for change in area's services (including districts)	- Prepare planning guidelines for districts - Set forward planning allocations	Collaborate with LAs Prepare new plans for area services	Review and approve district plans, and plans for area services
DISTRICT	Identify needs and opportunities for change in district's plans		Assist districts Roll forward and modify last year's district plans in light of guidelines, new allocation	

Prepare next-year budgets, etc.

Prepare next-year budgets, etc.

Prepare next-year budgets, etc.

4 years. When this has been done, DHSS staff will discuss and agree in broad terms with each RHA the changes in priorities or targets that they will introduce into their health service plan for the Region. These changes may be based on new departmental priorities or initiatives and on proposals by the RHA itself. At the same time DHSS will assign new provisional planning allocations of revenue and capital for the next 4 years to each RHA (together with an indication of what level of resources to assume up to Year 10). Thus the allocation process will become part and parcel of the process of agreeing on Authorities' future service development plans.

(2) RHAs will give planning guidance to AHAs

3.8.   Having agreed with DHSS on the changes to be introduced into their plans, and having been assigned a forward allocation of capital and revenue finance, RHAs will then undertake an essentially similar process with their AHAs. Thus they will determine, in the context of their agreement with DHSS, what changes to seek in the plans for their various Areas and Districts, and will discuss and agree them generally with each AHA. They will simultaneously indicate their provisional financial allocations to the AHAs, again extending 4 years ahead.

(3) AHAs will give planning guidance to Districts

3.9.   Having agreed with the RHA the lines on which their plans are to be modified, and having been assigned a provisional 4 year financial allocation, AHAs will then determine what consequential changes to seek in the plans for their Districts and in their Area-level services. The collaborative meetings with the matching local authority will be particularly useful at this point. In the same way as described above, they will then agree with each District the lines on which their plans require modification (again either at the initiative of the AHA or of the District itself).

(4) Plans will be prepared on a District basis

3.10.   District staff, in close co-operation with the Area Team of Officers and with its planning and information service, will then set about modifying and extending District plans, in the light of the availability of resources, agreed changes in priorities and targets, or changes in local circumstances. Within a District, initiatives for changes in the various parts of its plan should to a large extent be expected to come from the various standing or AD HOC planning teams.

(5) AHAs will review and approve District plans

3.11.   Districts' planning proposals will then be submitted to the AHA, to be reviewed by its Area Team of Officers, which will add material for Area-level services, and then to be considered by the AHA itself. This will be another point when the collaborative discussions with the local authority will be particularly important.

48

(6) RHAs will review and approve Area plans

3.12.   In a similar fashion the Regional Team of Officers will review each AHA's plan and add plans for Regional services, including the full Regional capital programme. The RHA will itself then consider the total plans and submit them to DHSS for approval (in the form of consolidated plans for the Region as a whole, with only a limited degree of District-by-District detail normally being presented).

(7) DHSS will review and approve Regional plans

3.13.   The final stage in the annual cycle will be the review and approval by DHSS of Regions' plans, the confirmation of definite financial allocations for the coming year and confirmed planning allocations for the following 3 years. DHSS will then consolidate the agreed Regional plans into a national picture of the way in which each service is expected to develop.

3.14.   Once new plans have been formulated and written up, it is likely to be difficult to insist on large-scale changes being introduced at this stage. Thus as between all management levels, it should be in the formulation and agreement on planning guidelines and in help during the preparation of plans, that one level exercises the most positive influence over the level below. The objective of these guidelines is thus to ensure, so far as possible, that the level below knows what priorities and targets are expected of it and where it will be able to introduce changes at its own discretion, without running the risk that these will prove unacceptable when they are finally presented.

B. COMPREHENSIVE DISTRICT HEALTH PLANS

3.15.   The basic management unit in the integrated NHS will be the District, defined as a population served by community health services supported by the specialist services of a district general hospital. The District is the lowest level at which it will be possible to make a comprehensive assessment of the health needs of the community, and to plan and deploy the broad range of health services required to meet these needs, and it will be at District level that clinicians will be directly involved in the planning process.

3.16.   Here and elsewhere, it is stressed that plans should be prepared on a District basis. It is hoped that plans will be developed by staff working at this level with guidance and help from Area, Region and Department. However, it would be naive to imagine that all Districts will immediately become fully competent in a difficult process. Thus higher levels must help develop this competence and, in the early years, provide it. Higher level plans will consist of a consolidation of lower level plans, together with plans for services provided at the higher level. Thus AHAs' plans will consist basically of plans for each of their Districts, with plans for Area-level services such as the school health service. Similarly, while RHAs should assemble Regional plans, these too should consist of a consolidation of plans for their Districts and Areas with plans for Regional services, and with a greater focus on the development of major building projects, for which RHAs carry primary responsibility.

3.17. To be effective and useful, the health plans prepared for each District will have to satisfy a number of requirements described below.

(1) They must cover all services and look up to 10 years ahead

3.18. Each District's plan should cover the whole range of the community's main needs for health care and of the services that are to be provided to meet these needs. A single "master plan" must therefore be prepared, that encompasses all of these aspects and places them within the context of the level of resources expected to be available to the District, identifying the total revenue expenditure, capital building and personnel requirements necessary to achieve the planned level of service.

3.19. Furthermore, planning and implementing significant changes in health services usually takes a number of years. District health plans should therefore extend forward to cover the full period within which it is necessary and realistic to plan for the future provision and improvement of the community's health service. This period varies depending upon the type of service involved; however, three periods can usefully be singled out.

a. *The short term*, within which it is possible to bring about changes through redeploying or changing the use of existing resources or changing working procedures.
b. *The medium term*, within which it is possible and realistic to estimate the resources that will be available, and plan their deployment, within the context of the constraints imposed by the existing major buildings etc. This period is about 4 years.
c. *The long term*, within which it is possible to implement radical changes in the District's health services—in particular, changes that require the design, building and commissioning of major new buildings. This period is about 10 years.

3.20. Thus the basic plan for the development of each District's health services should be drawn up for four years ahead, setting out for each year the estimated extent of the health needs of the different sections of the community, the deployment of the main services of each kind that will be provided to meet them, and the demands that these plans will put on the resources of skilled personnel, building and revenue finance (to match the revenue allocations assigned to the District). In addition, a long-term forward look to the Year 10 should be included, setting out, in more summary form, the main ways in which the District's health needs are expected to develop and the outline of the services to be provided to meet them, with particular attention to building and other requirements that must be planned well in advance (the capital programme being decided mainly at RHA level).

(2) They must plan for identified needs and explicit standards of service

3.21. Health services can only be evaluated in relation to the identifiable needs of the community for different kinds of health care, and, with integration, it will become possible for single management units to draw up health plans in this light. In practice, the health-care needs of the community are highly diverse and a single individual or family may simultaneously require health-care for several different conditions. However, it is useful for planning purposes to distinguish a limited number of broad "health-care groups" with special needs, and to differentiate some categories of care, such as specialties, so as to quantify the services required.

3.22. The concept of "health-care groups" has been presented in Chapter 1; examples are the care of elderly, maternity, mentally ill, mentally handicapped, acute secondary care, dental care etc.

3.23. The first step in developing a District plan will be to estimate the extent of local needs in such health-care categories. For this purpose, each District should have a defined population and area (or set of areas) assigned to it for each of the main specialties, for which population and area it will generally be responsible for providing health care in that specialty (without of course, implying that in individual cases patients will always be treated in the places that this would suggest). Ideally, each District would have a single population and area for all its specialties and services. In fact, it will be one of the objectives of the reorganised Health Service to develop, so far as is reasonable, a comprehensive health service within each District to meet the needs of its local community. At present, however, this ideal is seldom likely to be possible, especially for services involving large long-stay hospitals. Thus one District will frequently have to rely heavily upon long-stay psychiatric hospital facilities provided by another District or Area, while it may itself provide certain branches of acute secondary care to a wider population than its own. It will be the responsibility of RHAs and AHAs to assign such population and areas to each of their Districts and to ensure that they have adequate information on their population, its composition and likely future trends.

3.24. Secondly, the plans prepared should, so far as possible, be based on standards or targets for the level of care of all kinds to be provided to each of these health-care groups, in terms of the quantity of the services to be provided and, so far as is feasible, in terms of quality of care as well. At this point, the important thing is that the plan should be expressed in terms of whatever standards of care are chosen. Thus the first main section of the District health plan should contain an assessment of local needs and explicit standards of service.

(3) They must define the services to be provided to meet needs and standards

3.25. Although planning must start from the needs of the population, it must be expressed in terms of proposed developments of the component parts of the NHS to meet the required standards, for example, specialist services, nursing, or the ambulance service. An important characteristic of the Health Service is the intricate way in which a limited number of component services are combined to meet the needs of individuals. In some cases (e.g. dentistry) there is a reasonably clear correspondence between the need for care and the service provided to meet this need. In other cases (for example care of the elderly, or maternity), a wide range of different services are required to provide a complete programme of health care, including social services provided by the local authorities. This intricate inter-relationship between health needs and health services adds unavoidable complexity to the task of planning in the Health Service.

3.26. The second main section of the District health plan should draw together the implications of the needs established in the first part for the services

51

to be provided. It should set out how each service is to be developed, what changes in the quantity and use of resources (money, buildings, manpower, equipment) are planned, what changes in working procedures are necessary etc. These service plans will indicate the demands on basic resources to be made by proposed developments taking account of the likely availability of resources.

3.27.　Each District should therefore have a plan for the development of its services which is based on (but presented separately from) the plans for the main health-care groups.

(4) They must plan the use of basic resources

3.28.　Planning can only be realistic if it is conducted within the framework of the resources that are expected to be available, in particular revenue and capital finance (and the new facilities that can only be provided from capital finance), and the various types of skilled manpower that services require, notably medical and nursing staff. Thus having set out the planned development of each main service, the plans must identify the total demands that these put upon these resources and must have been prepared within the context of the level of these resources that is expected to be available (e.g. the forward revenue allocations assigned by the AHA to the District).

a. *Revenue costs.* District plans should estimate the expected total revenue costs of the services to be provided. These estimates do not need to be so detailed as the annual budgets prepared for the coming year and cannot be expected to be so accurate. However, they should be sufficiently sound to establish that the planned levels of service are realistic within the District's revenue allocations (and to assist the AHA in determining how revenue allocations should be reassigned among its Districts).

b. *Capital costs.* District plans should be framed within the context of the expected availability of capital facilities, based on the existing supply of hospital beds etc., and taking account of planned reductions and of the additions and replacements that can be envisaged from the Region and Area's capital budget. The strategy for scheduling the starts of major building projects will be largely the responsibility of the Region, based on the requirements identified by each of its Areas and Districts in their plans and formulated in consultation with them. Thus complete capital programmes need not form a part of the plan prepared at District level, but the consolidated Regional plans should be accompanied by a capital programme.

c. *Manpower.* Finally, District plans should include projections of the levels of skilled staff required to provide the planned levels of service—in particular, nursing and medical staff by specialty. As well as providing confirmation that the service plans developed are feasible from the manpower point of view, these manpower projections will provide the basis for planning the recruitment and training programmes necessary to ensure that the required supply of skilled manpower will be available when it is needed. They will also provide a basis for setting firm establishments for the coming year (as described below in the section on Personnel).

(5) They must define what needs to be done in the coming year

3.29. Finally, although planning must be concerned with the pattern of services to be provided some years in the future, its real value to management lies in the guidance it provides on what needs doing now, or during the coming year, to work towards this future pattern. The plans prepared must thus provide a basis for identifying what is to be done during the coming year, in terms of detailed budgets, establishments and performance targets for next year's regular operations. They must also define the other things that need to be done in order to achieve longer-term objectives—for example, what building work must be initiated, what cost-reduction exercises must be completed etc., and by whom within the organisation. These immediate action programmes are the real products of the planning process, and it is against these that actual performance can subsequently be monitored.

3.30. In summary, each District should have a comprehensive forward plan, setting out (as shown in Exhibit X):

a. The extent of the needs for health services of the different sections of the community or health-care groups, and the standards of care to be provided to these groups.
b. The resulting planned development of the major health services of the District to meet these needs, at the standard assumed within available resources.
c. The resulting required supply of skilled manpower, capital finance and revenue finance (to equal the forward allocations assigned to the District).
d. What needs doing during the coming year, in terms of budgets, establishments, other operating targets and "action programmes" to achieve longer term growth.

Section II—Monitoring and Control

3.31. Once the plans proposed by DMTs, AHAs and RHAs have been agreed, maximum authority will then be delegated to implement them. To maintain accountability upwards, it will be essential that performance is monitored and controlled in relation to these plans, to enable the next higher Authority to identify any unacceptable standards of service and efficiency and to seek corrective action in good time. Effective monitoring will serve a second purpose in that it will act as an incentive to maintain high standards, thereby preventing much of the need for intervention from higher up.

3.32. The first requirement for effective monitoring will be the existence of a plan to which each management level is committed. The plan will provide a yardstick against which to measure performance and will contain targets as incentives. The other requirements are:

a. the existence of adequate information about the service standards and efficiency of each management unit;
b. the effective use of this information to monitor these standards against plan;
c. the application of more specific controls over the use of resources such as finance and manpower.

EXHIBIT X

CONTENTS AND ARRANGEMENT OF DISTRICT PLAN

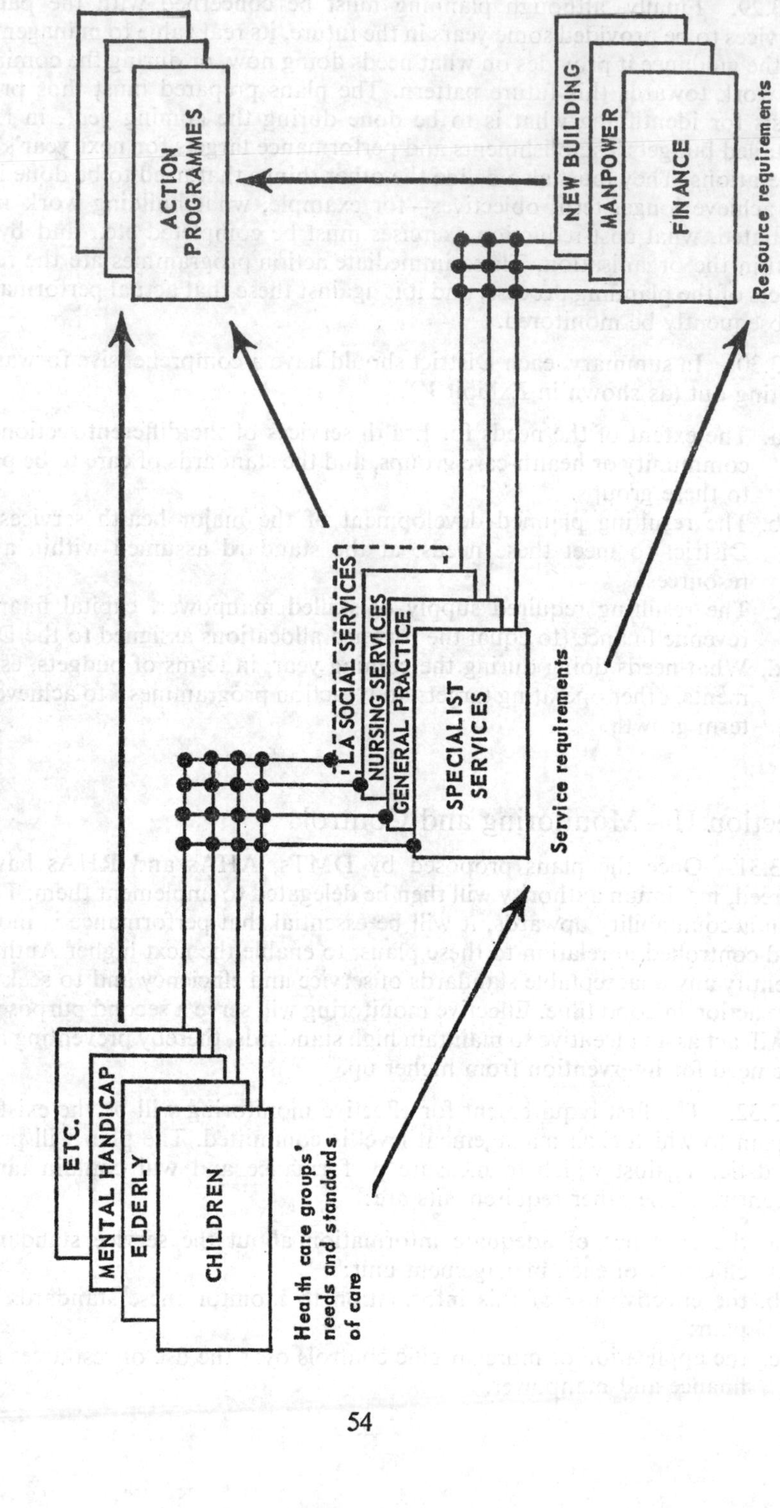

ACTION PROGRAMMES

NEW BUILDING

MANPOWER

FINANCE

Resource requirements

LA SOCIAL SERVICES

NURSING SERVICES

GENERAL PRACTICE

SPECIALIST SERVICES

Service requirements

ETC.

MENTAL HANDICAP

ELDERLY

CHILDREN

Health care groups' needs and standards of care

A. INFORMATION

3.33.   Information is required in the NHS for other purposes than monitoring by one level over another. Other uses are:

a. *day-to-day operations*; for example, information on patients, workload, personnel records etc;
b. *planning*; for example, information on the future size and composition of the District's population, on the development of its needs for different kinds of health services and on the future planning intentions of other agencies;
c. *information for use outside the immediate management context*; for example, information required by DHSS and other government departments for national policy-making purposes, or for national and international statistics.

3.34.   Although much information is available at all levels of the Service, many improvements will be needed. Existing information is sometimes unreliable, of doubtful relevance and out of date, and there are gaps in what is available, especially about the community's needs for health services and the effectiveness of services in meeting these needs. Improvements will take a long time to achieve, but the reorganisation of the Service provides the opportunity to set about the task. This should be done in two different ways:

a. *by a systematic assessment of what information is needed at each management level*, and by each function at these levels, for planning, for operations and for monitoring. For monitoring, this assessment should focus on what information is needed to measure the performance of each unit in relation to its plans, and in particular on useful measures of public needs and service effectiveness in meeting these needs;
b. *by the establishment of an expert information function at Area and Regional levels*. As a service to the officer team as a whole, this function would have the dual task of assisting responsible officers (for example, community physicians) to identify what information they require for different purposes and where this information might come from, and then of managing the process of gathering information, analysing it and presenting it in a form useful to those who need it.

3.35.   The task of improving the NHS's information system will require a co-ordinated effort, sponsored and promoted at the national level—but relying on the ideas and efforts of individuals at all levels in the Service—to develop improved basic information systems for establishment throughout the Service, in terms both of the information that should be available and the systems by which it should be retrieved, processed and presented.

B. USING INFORMATION FOR MONITORING

3.36.   Good information will not lead to effective monitoring unless positive use is made of it by each management level. One form of monitoring that is already carried out systematically throughout the Service is of expenditure against budget. This has been possible for three reasons: first, because budgets generally provide a good planning basis against which to assess performance; second, because the available accounting information is generally adequate as

55

a basis for assessing expenditure; and third, because finance officers and senior management have used this information systematically to check performance against budget and to intervene at as early a stage as possible to correct likely deviations.

3.37. The normal frequency for monitoring expenditure against budget is monthly. For monitoring performance against service standards a less frequent monitoring cycle will usually be sufficient, except where special attention is being focused upon a particular development. However, at least once a year, the Regional and Area Teams of Officers and DMTs should systematically evaluate the total performance of the AHAs, Districts, and services within Districts, to identify whether operating targets have been achieved, where the main gaps appear to be, why these gaps have developed and what should be done about it.

C. SPECIFIC CONTROLS

3.38. Specific controls relate to those decisions for which one management level must seek the approval of the next higher level. As such, the most important control used in the Service will be the review and approval of plans, followed by systematic monitoring of all aspects of performance in relation to plan. In addition however, a limited number of more specific controls will continue to need to be exercised, particularly in relation to the use of resources. The most important are controls over:

(1) revenue expenditure;
(2) capital expenditure and new building;
(3) certain aspects of Authorities' and Districts' organisation and management processes;
(4) establishments;
(5) staff pay and conditions of service.

The following paragraphs describe how the first three of these specific controls will be applied (the last two being described in Section III under Personnel Management).

(1) Revenue expenditure

3.39. To maintain financial accountability within the NHS, revenue expenditure during the year must continue to be closely controlled in relation to the agreed revenue budgets at each level. The aim of budgetary control is to ensure not only that total expenditure during the year matches the revenue resources available, but also that resources are used efficiently in relation to the results achieved. Financial control is therefore one part of the more general process of monitoring and controlling performance.

3.40. Budgets are built up from the estimates of expenditure on individual items such as wages and salaries and supplies of all kinds. But budgets only become a useful tool for control when such estimates are related to centres of specific responsibility for which individual Authorities, management levels or individual officers can be held responsible. Effective budgetary control will therefore depend on the clear assignment of responsibilities to specific management units or officers, on the allocation to them of budgets for the expenditure under their control and on their carrying the responsibility for controlling expenditure against their budgets.

3.41. The system of operating accounts and budgets will be revised to accord more closely with the responsibilities of specific management units and officers individually responsible within the new organisation. The system of budgeting and accounting will operate as follows:

a. Below District level, within institutions such as hospitals, the accounts and budgets will be framed to identify together the costs associated with particular departments or other centres of responsibility e.g. nursing. The responsible manager within the institution or service will help to draw up this part of the budget and will be held responsible for expenditure on all items in his budget.

b. At District level, budgets will then be consolidated under main headings; for example, for each institution, for the District nursing service and under the heads of the various District services.

c. At Area level, budgets will then be consolidated into budgets for each District, budgets for Area-level services (e.g. the ambulance service) and for the various Area headquarters' functions (e.g. the finance department). The AHA itself, assisted by the Area Team of Officers (particularly the Area Treasurer), will then focus their attention on expenditure under main headings, holding the officers of the DMTs and the Area officers accountable for controlling their expenditure within the budgets assigned to them.

d. Similarly, at Regional level, budgets will be consolidated into overall Area budgets and budgets for Regional services and headquarters' functions. The RHA and the Regional Team of Officers will then focus on expenditure under main headings, holding the AHAs and Regional-level service and function heads mainly responsible for controlling the expenditure within their agreed budgets.

3.42. Budgets having been developed and responsibilities assigned in this way, the stringency of financial control will depend on the detail in which budgets are controlled (i.e. under how many sub-headings expenditure is budgeted and monitored by the level above), the degree of freedom given for variation between headings and the extent to which reserves are provided at each level. A balance has to be drawn between the advantages of delegating authority downwards (which would imply a light control over expenditure within budgets of responsible managers) and the need to maintain accountability for public expenditure (which tends towards the reverse). The conflict between these two requirements will be minimised by assigning clear responsibility for expenditure to individual managers as described above. Subject to this, the following arrangements are proposed:

a. *Degree of detail in budgets.* Budgets have to be prepared and accounts kept to serve a wider purpose than simply financial control. For this latter purpose, the degree of detail in which one management level's expenditure is controlled by another should be kept to the minimum necessary to preserve financial accountability. The primary control will be over each unit's expenditure, primary responsibility for controlling items within this resting

57

with its manager or management group. Thus each level will monitor in less detail than the level below. There will also be a need to monitor the way in which expenditure is incurred to ensure that waste and extravagance are avoided and value for money obtained. But the higher the level the more selective will be the detail required.

b. *Controlling budget changes*. Since budgets are designed to provide resources to meet objectives within an agreed plan, departures from budget heads usually represent departures from plans. At the District management level, any proposals to switch expenditure between budget heads would have to be agreed with the AHA. In the absence of approval to change by the AHA, the DMT is bound by the approved plan and its budget.

c. *Holding of reserves*. The relative impact of unforeseen circumstances tends to be greatest at lower levels. Reserves can be held at any level in the Service, and the power to hold them and to allocate them at will is an important addition to delegated authority. It will be desirable that limited reserves be held at all three levels—Region, Area and District. The level of reserves held should be agreed as part of the approved plan and budget, and the use of such reserves should conform to the plan.

3.43. An important addition to the general discretion exercised by local management within the reorganised NHS will be achieved by two modifications to the procedures hitherto applied to the hospital service.

a. DHSS will permit the carry-over of a limited amount of unspent balances from one year to the next, subject to prescribed conditions.

b. There will also be authority, at the discretion of local management, to meet certain capital costs out of revenue (and perhaps the reverse), again subject to prescribed conditions.

(2) Control over capital expenditure and building

3.44. Authorities' capital expenditure within the year will be controlled to ensure that expenditure does not exceed budget and that it is applied to the agreed purposes. The procedure will be the same as that for controlling revenue expenditure. Thus it will be based on agreeing annual budgets, on monitoring expenditure against these budgets, and on the superior Authority's approval being necessary for the diversion of expenditure to other purposes during the year. It will also permit the carry-over of unspent balances, subject to prescribed conditions.

3.45. In addition however, there will be some control over the actual building schemes for which this money is allocated. This is described in Chapter 9.

(3) Control of Authorities' organisation and management procedures

3.46. Finally, there will be a continuing need for some central control over certain aspects of Authorities' organisation and management procedures. On the one hand, this will relate to such matters as the designation of private beds and other matters not directly affected by reorganisation. On the other hand, it will relate to matters directly connected with reorganisation—the general ways in which Authorities are organised and carry out their management tasks. In particular, RHAs, and if necessary DHSS, will have the power to approve AHAs' definition of Districts and their schemes of management.

Section III—Personnel Management

3.47. The NHS is one of the nation's largest employers of labour, much of it highly skilled. It currently employs more than 800,000 people—4 per cent of the working population—and wages and salaries account for almost 70 per cent of total current Health Service expenditure. Thus securing that staff can use their skills most effectively to achieve the objectives of the Health Service is one of the most important and most rewarding tasks of Health Service management. This is a major responsibility of managers in the hierarchically-organised professions (e.g. nursing) and in institutional services, and is often referred to as the personnel function. This function embraces the recruitment, development and management of staff; it includes all aspects of manpower information and planning; complementing, promotion and appointments arrangements; training and career development, with associated staff appraisal and counselling; negotiation of pay and other conditions of service and arrangements for consultation with staff interests and for the welfare of staff. It also includes the activities arising in the working situation such as consultation and grievance and disciplinary procedures.

3.48. Some of these activities will be carried out at national level, e.g. negotiation of pay and conditions of service. But most of the responsibility for personnel management will rest with professional staff and line managers working in the field. Thus the role specifications in Appendix 3 of Part II refer to the personnel management tasks of each manager. However, professional staff and managers will require specialist advice on some of the aspects of the personnel function. Some of this advice and support will come from fellow professionals. For example, medical administrators at Region or Area level will be involved in many aspects of personnel management for doctors, as will nursing staff for nurses. In addition, personnel officers at District, Area and Region will provide some general personnel services for all staff. These are also described in Part II of this report. This section describes the general personnel processes which underlie the proposed organisation. It covers, in turn, the arrangements for selecting and appointing staff, controlling establishment levels and staffing costs, and for management development in the NHS.

A. SELECTING AND APPOINTING STAFF

3.49. It will be for each employing Authority to operate selection procedures within national guidelines. These guidelines will cover methods of advertising, constitution of selection committees and the use of assessors, and they will be determined by the DHSS after consultation with the management, professional and staff interests and in the light of recommendations from staff advisory committees or similar machinery at national level.

3.50. The selection and appointment procedures will vary according to the category of staff and any relevant statutory provisions. But they must make it possible to satisfy the requisite standards expected by higher authority and professional groups, while at the same time enabling the immediate manager (where one exists) to participate directly in choosing the most acceptable applicant from among those who meet the policies and standards set. Officers with management

59

responsibilities can only reasonably be held accountable for the performance of their unit if they have a direct say in the selection of their staff.

3.51.   The selection process for specified categories of hierarchically-organised staff (i.e. where managers are accountable for the work of their subordinates) will therefore take place in two stages:

   a. *Creation of a final short list.* This will be carried out in a series of steps, in the course of which applicants who are judged not to meet requisite standards will be screened out by the manager once removed* and by assessors. The steps may include preliminary screening of written applications and in some cases interviews of candidates with the help of assessors.
   b. *Selection.* This will usually occur at a selection board, which may include Members and/or officers, as well as assessors where appropriate. The manager of the officer to be appointed will participate and normally no appointment will be made which is unacceptable to him.†

3.52.   Arrangements will also differ according to the level of post to be filled. Thus:

   a. *Employing Authorities* will be directly involved in the selection of senior staff. This group includes consultants, chief nursing officers and heads of paramedical departments where the paramedical specialist is a direct adviser to the consultant or GP e.g. biochemist or physicist, or where there is no appropriate consultant or GP to manage the service.
   b. *Senior officers of the Authority* will normally have delegated powers‡ for selecting and appointing their immediate subordinates, providing that the post already exists.§
   c. *Similarly, certain subordinate managers* will select staff to fill vacancies from a short list, with the assistance of assessors as appropriate.

3.53.   Finally, the nationally-determined procedures (see paragraph 3.49) should also provide for employing Authorities and managers in the Health Service to initiate the redeployment and reallocation of duties of their staff according to the needs of the Service and an officer's performance. This should be made clear in contracts of employment. Safeguards against personal hardship or injustice will need to form a part of the procedures.

B. CONTROLLING ESTABLISHMENTS AND STAFFING COSTS

3.54.   Previous sections of this Chapter have described how manpower plans will be developed at District level and how requirements for additional staff will be incorporated into AHA and RHA plans. This section describes how, in the reorganised Service, staffing levels and costs will be controlled and a balanced

---

   * The manager once removed is the manager of the immediate superior of the post to be filled, e.g. in the present nursing structure a Chief Nursing Officer is often the manager once removed of a Senior Nursing Officer.
   † Arrangements will need to be made to ensure that the overwhelming advice of assessors is not ignored by managers—though this is most unlikely to happen.
   ‡ This power will need to be delegated in writing, with the post and/or managerial levels clearly specified.
   § I.e. is included within the agreed establishment.

distribution of staff secured between different specialities and locations. Four separate tasks are involved:

(1) *Negotiate pay and conditions of service for all new working levels* within the reorganised Health Service.
(2) *Determine 1974–1975 establishment and manpower budget for each new statutory Authority*, by agreeing total staff inventory on vesting day and management organisation (including levels of responsibility) as soon as possible thereafter.
(3) *Control staffing levels and costs after 1974*, by reviewing in detail any requests for, and increases in, senior medical/dental and other specified posts.
(4) *Ensure that national agreements for pay and conditions of service are implemented locally*, by exercising control over variations.

Each of these tasks, and the role of the different levels in the reorganised Health Service in carrying them out, is discussed below.

(1) Negotiating pay and conditions of service for new posts

3.55. The management organisations will need to differ between AHAs and between Districts in order to meet local requirements. However, there is a relatively small number of new categories of posts to be created in all Areas and Districts. But there will be considerable variation in the permutation and combination of such posts. Appendix 3 to Part II of this report contains role specifications for new posts arising from the proposed NHS management structure. These role specifications indicate the managerial level of each post.*

3.56. For every new category of post it will first be necessary to define the work to be done and the managerial level, and then to decide the pay and conditions of service appropriate to each. Grading divisions within managerial levels will often be needed to reflect the different responsibilities carried by officers of the same levels in different situations. Pay and conditions of service will, of course, be determined at national level through the accepted negotiating machinery.

(2) Establishing initial manpower budgets

3.57. Once pay and conditions of service for new posts are agreed, control over initial establishment levels and staffing costs will be secured by drawing up a manpower budget for 1974–1975 for each new statutory Authority. This budget will reflect the establishment level and management organisation against which future changes can be controlled. Three separate steps are involved in establishing the first manpower budget for each new Authority.

a. *Carry out (during 1973)† an inventory of all non-clinical, non-managerial staff* (e.g. first-line supervisors and below) forecast to be in post on 1 April 1974. The initial establishment levels will thus be those that obtain on

---

* The introduction to Appendix 3 defines "managerial level". If two officers are to be in a manager–subordinate relationship, they must be of different managerial levels.

† This may be over-optimistic; but this task will need to be one of the first responsibilities of shadow Authorities when they are established.

vesting day. Each shadow AHA will therefore need to draw up a detailed statement of the numbers (whole-time equivalents) of staff in each major function (catering, domestic, portering etc), that it will inherit from the Authorities (local authorities, RHBs, BGs, HMCs and Executive Councils) at present providing health services in the Area. The DHSS will determine the level of detail required.

b. *Similarly, identify numbers of consultants, junior hospital doctors, salaried dentists, paramedical staff and nurses for each new Authority.* Shadow RHAs and AHAs will also need to forecast the numbers, broken down by rank and speciality, of clinical staff that they will inherit from the present Authorities.

c. *Develop and agree the detailed management organisation of each new Authority.* Shadow AHAs will need to determine (in consultation with shadow local authorities) District boundaries and propose detailed schemes of management which will show how the principles of the management arrangements agreed by the Secretary of State will be applied locally. These schemes will extend at least to two levels below the District Management Team or Area Team of Officers (e.g. to include senior nursing officers, sector administrators, District catering officers) and they will propose a precise managerial level and grading division for each post. A detailed role specification will be prepared for all senior posts. Schemes of management will be reviewed and agreed during the run-up to April 1974 (or as soon as possible thereafter) as follows:

DHSS will review, evaluate and approve schemes of management developed by shadow RHAs.

Shadow RHAs will review and evaluate schemes of management developed by shadow AHAs (including plans for establishing Districts and setting up District Management Teams) and submit them to the DHSS for approval* where necessary.

3.58.   Thus during early 1974, there will be, for each new Authority, agreed statements of staffing levels for medical, dental, paramedical and nursing staff by specialty, and for non-management support staffs, and the details of the management organisation will have been developed, reviewed and agreed. These statements can then be costed out and 1974–1975 manpower budgets prepared for each new Authority, which can be checked against national estimates.

(3) Controlling changes in staffing levels and costs

3.59.   Once initial establishments and management organisations have been agreed, it will be possible to exercise control over any subsequent changes through the annual planning and budgeting process. Thus:

a. *Establishments for all staff, other than medical, dental, paramedical and managerial staff,* will be controlled by means of the annual District, Area or Regional health plan and its associated budget. As mentioned earlier in this Chapter, this plan will:

* It will be for the DHSS to decide the level of detail in AHA schemes of management which it wishes to review.

Identify and justify any significant changes in establishment levels proposed during the planning period, for each major function.

Translate establishment levels into manpower budgets, which can then be compared with previous years and with proposals in other similar Districts, Areas and Regions.

Thus the main control over numbers of non-clinical, non-managerial staffs will be financial. So long as local managers provide the agreed level of service within the agreed costs and budgets and follow national personnel policies, it will be up to them to decide the staffing and internal organisation of their departments, and higher authority need not intervene.

b. *Medical, and some paramedical, staffing establishments* will need more detailed control. Planning targets drawn up on the advice of the Central Manpower Committee will, among other things, include appropriate ratios of training to consultant posts. The number of doctors, dentists and some paramedical staff is constrained by the training places available, and there will be a continuing need to promote a more even distribution of staff between Areas and between medical (and some paramedical) specialties. It is therefore proposed that:

AHAs should include in their annual health plans any proposals for increasing medical or paramedical posts. These proposals will stem from agreed District plans.

RHAs will be able to approve, as part of the annual planning process, new appointments for junior hospital doctors (within guidance to be provided by the Central Manpower Committee) and for most senior paramedical staff, provided the costs can be absorbed within the agreed AHA budget. The DHSS will review RHA proposals for increases in senior medical and dental and selected* paramedical establishments contained in Regional health plans. Allocation will then be made by DHSS en bloc to RHAs, and each RHA will decide how the Region's increase in a particular grade or specialty should be apportioned among its AHAs.

c. *Managerial† staffing levels* will be controlled by a requirement that any change from the agreed management organisation must be reviewed and agreed (paragraph 3.57 above) as part of the annual planning process. Thus the agreed management organisation and establishment levels will continue to operate unless and until changes are proposed and agreed by the next higher Authority. This means that for changes to the agreed District management organisation (including changes to managerial levels or grades):

AHAs will review and evaluate any District proposals and incorporate agreed changes in the annual plan for agreement by the RHA.

RHAs will agree changes in AHA organisation, provided that funds are available to meet the costs involved. The DHSS must be informed of any changes approved by the Region and may in the initial stages wish to approve these.

* E.g. because there is a national shortage of the staff in question, or because distribution between Regions is uneven and national policy is to seek to correct the imbalance.
† Which will include senior nursing staff.

The DHSS will review, evaluate, and agree all changes proposed to RHA management organisation, and the Department will monitor changes in AHA organisation approved by RHAs.

3.60. Because staffing questions are so important to the effectiveness of the Service in meeting patient needs, and because wages and salaries are so large an element in total costs, decisions to recommend changes in establishment levels will normally be taken by District Management Teams and Area and Regional Teams of Officers. But they will be supported by specialist personnel departments at both Area and Region (described in Chapter 11) and by a strengthened NHS personnel function within the DHSS.

(4) Ensuring observation of national agreements on pay and conditions

3.61. Once agreement has been reached at national level on pay and conditions of service, steps must continue to be taken to see that what has been agreed is implemented locally.

a. *The DHSS will issue circulars setting out the terms of agreements* and it will be the responsibility of Authorities and their managers to see that they are implemented. These will be monitored and the need for corrective action (if any) identified through internal NHS auditing procedures.

b. *The DHSS will continue to authorise local variations from national agreements* (where these do not cover a particular local situation), at least in the period immediately following NHS reorganisation. Longer term however, once specialist personnel departments are effectively established at RHAs, authority to agree local variations may in some cases be delegated to RHAs by the DHSS, within clearly established guidelines. But the DHSS must continue to be informed, by means of copies of letters or an annual statistical return, when variations are agreed, since the need to authorise variations to an agreement is important evidence as to the effectiveness of the agreement itself in meeting Service needs.

C. DEVELOPING MANAGERS IN THE NHS

3.62. If the proposed management organisation for the NHS is to be effective in its ultimate aim of securing improvements to health care for patients, highly skilled and experienced managers will be needed at all levels of organisation and in many functions. The development of managerial skill is a continuous process, involving formal professional and management training and experience in a variety of different jobs. This section describes the main management training tasks in the NHS and outlines the steps to be taken to ensure that managers receive the career experience needed to fit them for senior posts in the Service.

(1) Management training in the NHS

3.63. Management training in the Health Service will continue to build on the existing professional and management training programmes, which cover both entry and post-entry training. Much of this training falls within nationally-determined patterns. In recent years, a number of reports have recommended systematic training arrangements for particular staff groups in order to secure the required succession of competent staff.

3.64. Developing the management potential of their subordinates is a responsibility of all officers in the Health Service. They will be assisted by specialist personnel departments at Regional, Area and (sometimes, depending upon its size) District level, in three important ways:

a. *Assisting with agreed staff appraisal procedures.* Unless the management potential of employees is identified and their development as managers monitored, there is a risk that talent will be wasted or that officers will be promoted too fast for their own good or that of the Service. Personnel departments at Area and Region will assist managers to introduce and maintain comprehensive staff appraisal procedures.

b. *Providing career guidance for administrative, finance and works staff.* Most advice on an officer's future career must continue to come from his immediate superior and colleagues and the head of his profession in his Authority. But in the new situation that will exist after 1974, managers themselves will wish to have expert advice to draw on. This advice will be provided by the RHA and AHA personnel departments. These will be able to build on the work pioneered by the National Staff Committee and extended thereafter in Regions. Moreover, personnel departments will from time to time receive advice from DHSS on career guidance and other personnel questions, following recommendations from the staff advisory committees at national level.

c. *Arranging training programmes.* RHA and AHA personnel officers will work with managers to identify the particular management training needs of individual members of their staff. In the light of national advice, they will arrange courses with local Colleges or Universities and maintain contact with other Health Authorities and the DHSS to make use of national training facilities. When necessary they will hold courses and seminars themselves.

(2) Provide career experience for potential managers

3.65. Ability to plan an officer's career through his service is an essential corollary of management training and a necessary prerequisite for developing effective senior managers. "Planned movement", as it has become known, has proved difficult to sustain in the hospital service partly because of the number and limited size of many employing Authorities. The reorganisation of the Health Service will substantially reduce the number of employing Authorities, and three steps can help to develop the concept of planned movement of staff:

a. *Appointing officers to a grade rather than to a particular post.* This will, with appropriate safeguards, facilitate transfer of administrative staff between functions within one Authority. Thus an administrator (for example), with the necessary qualifications and experience, could work successively, if he so wishes, in, say, a Family Practitioner Committee and an Area personnel department before being appointed a sector administrator, without having to move from Area to Area to gain the necessary experience to equip him for senior posts.

b. *Encouraging Authorities to develop the management potential of their own staff.* Each Authority should seek to identify and develop the management potential of its present staff rather than rely on attracting substantial numbers of trained staff from elsewhere, and one of the criteria for advancement of administrative staff should be demonstrated ability to identify and develop the management potential of staff. This will help to encourage Authorities to devote more attention to recruitment policies and management training* and will reduce the need for staff to move continuously round the country if they want to advance within the Service. As manpower policies are developed, it should be feasible to determine the need for, including the extent of, advertisement of vacancies at the various levels.

c. *Assigning some career development responsibilities to personnel officers at Area and Region.* One of the specific tasks of Area and Regional personnel officers should be to ensure that potential managers have the opportunity to develop their managerial skills. For this purpose, personnel officers should negotiate moves for individuals (with the agreement of the individuals concerned) within an Authority, in accordance with an agreed career plan.

3.66. These procedures depend on effective personnel departments at Area and Region to complement the strengthened personnel function within the DHSS. The role and the organisation of these personnel departments are described in Chapter 11 of this report.

---

* A recent survey showed that less than half the existing hospital Authorities have responded to the invitation in HM(68)96 to make an officer specifically responsible for training, and where such an officer has been appointed he rarely works full time on training and is rarely specially trained for the task.

Part II
Organisation of Skill Groups

CHAPTER 4
DOCTORS IN MANAGEMENT

4.1.   Health services are heavily dependent on the dedication of doctors and the other healing professions. Doctors rely on sound management of the NHS to enable them to serve their patients more effectively and administrators and the management structure are there to support them in their work. So close is this inter-relationship that medical participation is essential in the management of the Service at all levels. This cannot be casual or conflicting but must be woven into the main design. Two kinds of direct medical participation are needed:

a. Doctors giving personal clinical services must bring to management accurate knowledge of current clinical activities, which largely determine the quantity and quality of calls made upon the Service. Resources to meet these calls are limited, and clinicians must therefore help to determine priorities among competing or conflicting claims and recommend and put into practice new ways of making the most of resources available. The first section of this Chapter discusses this issue.

b. The other kind of direct medical contribution will be provided by specialists in community medicine, who will be involved full-time in the planning and organisation of health services and in the provision of general preventive, screening and clinic services. They will be part of the management structure and their particular skills and knowledge have been reviewed in detail in the recent report of the Working Party on Medical Administrators (Chairman, Dr R B Hunter). The second section of this Chapter outlines how their skills will be employed in the reorganised NHS, taking into account also the recommendations of the Working Party on Collaboration. It also refers to the doctors performing clinical work in the public health field and at present accountable to the Medical Officer of Health or Principal School Medical Officer.

4.2.   The organisation appropriate for the one does not apply to the other, but the aim of both groups is the same and clinicians and specialists in community medicine have important, complementary and interdependent parts to play.

4.3.   In addition to direct participation at the local level in the management process, doctors giving personal clinical service will contribute to management in two other ways. The first is as appointed Members of Health Authorities. The second is through the medical advisory committees which will play an important part in the planning process at these levels. It is still an open question whether

67

doctors appointed as Members of an Authority can also be members of management teams jointly responsible to that Authority.

A. THE CLINICIAN'S ROLE IN THE MANAGEMENT PROCESS

4.4.　The first duty of a clinician is to practise clinical medicine. But in doing so, every doctor makes demands upon resources, which have to be reconciled one with another, and his clinical actions interact in complex ways with the work of others, in both the health and personal social services. Clinicians are important innovators and their ideas must be picked up by management, upon which they therefore unavoidably make an impact. The benefits of this impact will be greatest (and the ill-effects least), if the clinicians can:
   a. take an active part in the management process;
   b. carry out their clinical duties with an understanding of the effects on other parts of the Service;
   c. be committed to proposed changes and developments.

4.5.　There is need, however, to evolve ways in which clinicians can participate in management effectively, without too great a diversion of their time and energies. This is best done through representative committees. It is, therefore, proposed that in each District clinicians should form a District Medical Committee of representatives based on specialty or other groupings.*

4.6.　In an integrated Service the parts played in management by clinicians working in hospitals and in general practice will be equally important, despite the fact that their contracts and organisation will be different. For instance, general practitioners will be under contract for the provision of general medical services with the Family Practitioner Committee, whilst consultants will have contracts of employment with the RHA or AHA(T). Both general practitioners and consultants exercise clinical autonomy† and are consequently their own managers. General practitioners manage their practice affairs and lay staff and this may at times include managing a trainee practitioner or assistant. Consultants will also manage their affairs and their subordinate medical staff, who will mainly be in training grades. Consultants by the nature of their work will have a greater need to co-ordinate their demands on resources than general practitioners, who must, however, also be given an equal opportunity to influence changing policies which can affect their mode of work and potential load.

(1) The District Medical Committee

4.7.　The District Medical Committee (DMC), which should represent all general practitioners and hospital doctors and co-ordinate the medical aspects of health care throughout the District, should be fairly small, usually about a dozen. Each member would represent a group of doctors with common interests. The DMC would elect not more than two representatives (who might be chairman and vice-chairman) on to the District Management Team (DMT). Initially

* The experience gained in recent years in hospital management has been useful in proving that suitably motivated representative committees based on functional groupings of doctors ("divisions") can be very successful.
† The expression "clinical autonomy" is explained in paragraph 2.3 of Chapter 2.

one representative should be chosen from general practice and the other from hospital practice, but both would be concerned with the whole range of medical matters. (The District Community Physician, whose role is fully described later, will have much to offer the DMC. He should attend meetings, ex officio, as of right and will be able to provide information and assist in its interpretation. Consideration should also be given to inviting the District Administrator and District Nursing Officer to attend meetings as appropriate.)

4.8.   The DMC will have both advisory and executive roles. It will make recommendations to the DMT based on the medical consensus view of priorities and plans. It will use its authority as a self-regulating body to persuade individual clinicians to co-operate in the implementation of plans agreed by the consensus. Its functions will therefore include:

   a. Arriving at a consensus view on medical policies and priorities.
   b. Considering opportunities to improve or develop medical services, especially involving co-operation among different specialties, and acting as the forum for agreement between consultants and general practitioners.
   c. Endorsing the medical view expressed by doctors on health-care planning teams.
   d. Ensuring that agreed policies and plans are communicated to individual consultants and general practitioners and persuading them to follow the consensus view.
   e. Using persuasion to influence expenditure on certain budget items such as drugs, surgical supplies etc.

(2) Role of DMC members of DMTs

4.9.   The chairman and vice-chairman will lead the proceedings and activities of the DMC, and in so doing will express their personal views as well as those of the specialty grouping to which they belong.

4.10.   As full members of the DMT, the DMC representatives will take part in all its discussions and decisions. As team members they are parties to the consensus decisions of the team and share in its collective duties and joint responsibility. But unlike other members of the DMT, they take their places not as heads of hierarchically-organised professions but as elected representatives of equals. They must enjoy the confidence of their colleagues, so that they can speak for clinicians not as mere delegates, unable to commit their peers without reference back, but as representatives using the discretion vested in them as a basis for action. Only when clinicians give and accept the confidence of their colleagues in this way can they collectively play their full part in management decisions, many of which concern them vitally.

4.11.   These representatives are active clinicians and their continuing credibility as representatives rests on this fact. They will therefore be able to spare only a part of their time for the business of the DMC and the DMT. Moreover, they should not hold office on the DMC for too long; perhaps five years is as much as most of them will want to serve. Their terms of office should be staggered to ensure continuity of thought, both on the DMC and DMT.

4.12.   In these respects the DMC representatives differ from the other medical member of the team, the District Community Physician, who deploys special skills and whose post affords him detailed knowledge of the health circumstances of the District. However, he will not expect to give clinical advice and is not empowered to speak for clinicians (see para 4.24 *et seq*). The roles of DMC representatives and of District Community Physician are therefore complementary and mutually reinforcing, giving medical advice and commitment across the whole field of District services.

(3) The representative structure

4.13.   The DMC has been described as comprising representatives of specialty groupings of doctors in the District. The composition of these groupings will depend on local needs and preferences. But it appears from preliminary discussions that in many Districts the medical staff will wish to be represented in groupings similar to "Cogwheel"* divisions. Each grouping would elect a representative on to the DMC.

4.14.   A method is needed to elect general practitioner representatives on to the DMC in equitable numbers. Various ways have been suggested:
  a. Groupings of general practitioners might be formed in the District and each might elect its representative to the DMC. Since general practitioners have a common functional interest, these groupings would presumably be geographically determined.
  b. The Local Representative Committee, recognised by the Family Practitioner Committee (FPC) as representing the general medical practitioners of the Area, might nominate members to each DMC from the doctors practising in the District concerned.

4.15.   The DMC might also contain representatives of junior doctors, certain specialised groups, such as the clinical doctors who have been working in the local authority services, and of dental practitioners, all of whom will certainly have an interest in the affairs of the functional or specialty groupings from which the DMC derives. Such a committee might be unduly comprehensive for some business and it may be thought necessary to form a sub-committee to co-ordinate the specialist divisions. Here much of the work currently done in hospital Medical Executive Committees could be carried out but even so some cross-representation from general practice is desirable. A parallel sub-committee for general practice might also be useful. Since an important aim of NHS reorganisation is to integrate and unify the Service, these sub-committees will not be rival factions but complementary offshoots of the united parent DMC in which the different medical disciplines play equal, co-operative parts.

(4) Medical advisory machinery

4.16.   Although the structure and functions of medical advisory committees do not directly concern the management study they will be an important means by which the local clinicians can be consulted by the Area and Regional Authorities and their officers on crucial planning issues. The Committees must therefore be not only representative but balanced, so as to provide the best possible advice in the local circumstances.

* Divisions of diagnostic services, geriatrics, medicine, obstetrics and gynaecology, psychiatry, and surgery (including dental surgery) are those most often seen in current hospital practice though there are many local variations.

4.17. In Areas of two or more Districts, these committees will be separate from the District organisation already described although no doubt partly derived from it. In an Area without a District (or a "single-District" Area) one single Area Medical Committee would fulfil the functions of both the DMC and the Area Medical Advisory Committee. For the latter role the membership may have to be augmented to ensure that Regional specialties active in the particular Area are covered.

B. COMMUNITY MEDICINE

4.18. The report of the Hunter Working Party on Medical Administrators has reviewed in detail the work of specialists in community medicine. This section outlines the ways in which their skills will be employed in the reorganised NHS. It is in two parts dealing with:
(1) The role in general of the specialist in community medicine.
(2) The role at different levels.
   —The District Community Physician.
   —The Area Medical Officer.
   —The Regional Medical Officer.

(1) Role of the specialist in community medicine

4.19. The specialist in community medicine must be more than an adviser. As argued in the Hunter Report, he must be a part of the management structure. Hence at all levels he will be an officer of the relevant Authority. He must be a member of the multi-disciplinary team at each level—District, Area and Region—since his specialist training is directly related to the work of these teams. Thus the specialist in community medicine will strengthen the team's competence in planning services, establishing health-care priorities and allocating resources, through his knowledge of community needs and the effectiveness of existing services. Like the other officers of the team he will be held accountable for meeting objectives related to the functions delegated to him. He will contribute to consensus decisions and share in the joint responsibility of the team.

4.20. A specialist in community medicine has three main functions; as a specialist, as an accountable manager, and as an adviser to and a manager of services for local government. But it must be made clear that in none of these roles does he have managerial authority over doctors giving personal clinical services.

Role as a specialist

4.21. A specialist in community medicine must stimulate the process of integration. He will provide a service to clinicians, acting as an additional link between them, and also as a link with the local authority services. He will assist clinicians by providing them with information on needs and advice on the effectiveness of alternative approaches to care.

71

Role in management

4.22.   There are four main aspects of his role in management:

a. *Planning*

In the reorganised Health Service there will be greater emphasis on planning to improve and develop health-care services and to help achieve the best use of resources. The decisions on which plans to adopt and which priorities to recommend will be a team activity, but the planning responsibilities of each team member must be defined clearly. Doctors, both clinicians and specialists in community medicine, must play a fundamental part in the planning of operational* health services. Clinicians will be engaged in planning through the DMC and its constituent divisions, through the health-care planning teams (see paragraph 2.48) and at Area and Region through the medical advisory machinery. Although the planning task will be different at the different levels, at each the specialist in community medicine will draw together the planning work of clinicians and will also contribute his epidemiological and other knowledge of local health circumstances. He will thus be accountable for the formulation and content of operational health-care plans. He will also be accountable for co-ordinating the activities of the other team members involved in the particular project and for seeing that the related operational and supporting services are complementary to it. He will often do this by co-ordinating the work of multidisciplinary planning teams.

b. *The development and interpretation of information*

Information of many kinds will be required by the team to make effective decisions, and the community medicine specialist will be one source of information. He will also have a role in designing information systems and providing the team and others with medical intelligence, e.g. analysis of needs, performance information and comparative analysis of different approaches to care. He will see that information on health care available to the team and others is of appropriate quality and relevance, and will play an important role in the interpretation of information.

c. *The evaluation of service effectiveness*

The specialist in community medicine will review relevant information on the provision of health care and assess the adequacy of that care, both in relation to needs and to possible alternative approaches. Such evaluation will often entail monitoring the implementation of plans or improvement projects, but it will not be in any way a clinical audit nor interfere with the clinical autonomy of individual clinicians.

d. *Co-ordination of preventive care services, and the deployment of clinical doctors in public health*

At Area and District level, the specialist in community medicine will have particular responsibilities for co-ordinating preventive services, including vaccination, immunisation, screening, health education and chiropody. The specialist in community medicine will be responsible for ensuring that preventive services are available for the population as a whole, although some of these services will be increasingly provided by general practitioners with the attached health visitors and nursing staff.

* "Operational" services have a medical content, as distinct from "support" services, e.g. laundries.

72

Role in relation to local authorities

4.23.   A more detailed working out of the functions of the specialist in community medicine in relation to local government will be found in the Collaboration Working Party reports and in circulars of guidance to be issued subsequently. A summary is included here to indicate the management arrangements to be made by the NHS to ensure that adequate advice and services can be given to matching local authorities in three main areas of work; environmental health, child health including school health, and personal social services.

a. *Environmental health.*

   Depending on the characteristics of the Area, either the District Community Physician or the Area Medical Officer (or one of his subordinates) will be appointed by the local authority as proper officer responsible for environmental health.*

b. *School health service.*

   The Area Medical Officer, or more usually a specialist in community medicine on his staff with a functional responsibility for child and school health as a whole, will be the adviser to the local education authority. The District Community Physician may carry out functions in relation to the school health service in accordance with policies agreed at AHA level under the direction of the Area Medical Officer and/or his child health specialist subordinate.

c. *Personal social services.*

   The Area Medical Officer, or a specialist in community medicine on his staff, will be responsible for advising the matching local authority.

(2) Role at different levels

4.24.   The precise nature of the job to be done by the specialist in community medicine will be different at the different levels and these are considered below.

District Community Physician

4.25.   The District Community Physician (DCP) will be a member of the DMT, which differs (except in the "single-District" Area) from teams at other levels by the inclusion of the two elected clinicians. These three doctors will have complementary roles and will work in mutual support. The District is the primary level of integration and District planning will play a major role in its achievement. The DCP will normally have functional co-ordinating responsibilities for health-care service planning (as described in paragraph 4.22a). In particular he will:

---

* In AHAs which are coterminous with metropolitan districts, and in AHAs which are coterminous with non-metropolitan counties but which have no health Districts, the Area Medical Officer or a member of his headquarter staff would be the proper officer.

In AHAs coterminous with non-metropolitan counties where there are health Districts, the appropriate District Community Physician would be the proper officer to the local government districts. Finally, in AHAs coterminous with metropolitan districts which have health Districts, e.g. Birmingham, the District Community Physician might have functions within the field of environmental health, but the Area Medical Officer and not he would be the proper officer to the metropolitan district.

73

a. *Identify opportunities to improve the operational health-care services* so as to enable the best patient care to be provided with the resources available. He will continuously assess the community's need, maintain a health profile and keep the provision of services under review to identify gaps in relation to need.

b. *Co-ordinate the work of the health-care planning teams*, including drawing up plans for the DMT and evaluating the effectiveness of changes made.

c. *Co-ordinate preventive services in the District*, including maintaining operational control of clinical doctors in public health attached by the AMO to him (see paragraph 4.31).

d. *Advise his consultant and general practitioner colleagues* as a specialist in community medicine, making available his knowledge of the District and his expertise in the organisation of health care, and assist the DMC, particularly in relation to presentation and interpretation of medical intelligence.

4.26. In some Areas he may act as the proper officer to the local authority on matters relating to environmental health and may also perform functions in relation to the school health service.

4.27. There will only be one DCP but he will receive support from specialists in community medicine on the AMO's staff who have specialised fields of interest. In certain circumstances he may need to be assisted by an additional specialist or specialists in community medicine at District level, in which case special local arrangements will be made. He will also be assisted by an administrator, attached to him by the District Administrator, whose primary role will be to give him support and also to support the health-care planning teams in the District.

4.28. The DCP, as a member of the DMT, will be directly accountable to the AHA. In this capacity he will be subject to the monitoring and co-ordinating authority of the Area Team of Officers. Thus the Area Team of Officers, and the AMO in particular, will review District health-care plans, ensuring that they conform to established Area policies and priorities, and will monitor District performance. The DCP may also have functions, in relation to those aspects of the school health service for which the local authority remains responsible, assigned to him by the AMO as the medical adviser of the local authority. For these specific local authority functions (and for these purposes only) the DCP will be responsible, not to the AHA, but directly to the AMO. Finally, when the DCP acts as proper officer to a local authority district on environmental health, he will be directly accountable to that district authority.

Area Medical Officer

4.29. The Area Medical Officer (AMO) will be a member of the Area Team of Officers. As a member of the team he will share responsibility for advising the AHA, establishing guidelines for district planning, reviewing District plans, and monitoring and co-ordinating DMT's performance. His particular responsibilities regarding these team functions will be to:

a. *Advise the team on health-care policies* after review of national and Regional policy initiatives, policy proposals submitted by District management and the matching local authorities.

74

b. *Recommend to the team District planning guidelines* on health-care policies, priorities and allocation of resources. He will later review the operational health-care aspects of the District planning proposals against these guidelines.
c. *Assist the team to monitor and co-ordinate the performance* of District management, particularly in relation to the functions of the DCP.

4.30.   In addition, the AMO will co-ordinate the planning of operational health-care services with the matching local authority, both through the joint consultative committees and by other less formal means.

4.31.   In addition to these team responsibilities, the AMO will also have duties as an individual, such as to:
a. *Advise the AHA on how to use their medical advisory machinery effectively,* convening specialist advisory groups, if necessary, in consultation with the Medical Advisory Committee.
b. *Promote research and studies* related to the delivery and organisation of health care and the development of information systems.
c. *Co-ordinate child health services,* including the school health services, throughout the Area and provide advice to the education authority, or, with the agreement of the education authority, appoint a senior member of his staff for the purpose.
d. *Advise the local authority social services department.*
e. *Organise the development of clinical doctors in public health.* These clinical doctors are at present employed by local authorities to do clinical work for infants, pre-school children and in the school health service, but they are also concerned with family planning and screening. They are hierarchically organised, exercising professional discretion. In the reorganised NHS, they will be on the staff of the AMO and deployed by him to continue their present work. They may work at District level under the operational control of the DCP.

4.32.   In an AHA(T) the AMO will provide certain personnel services for consultants and senior registrars in relation to their contracts. In all AHAs however, he will have personnel duties for medical staff below senior registrar.

4.33.   The AMO will have a number of specialists in community medicine on his headquarters staff, who will be accountable to him. The number will vary according to the population served and its health and social characteristics. The specialists will have functional responsibilities as follows:
a. A specialist responsible for service planning, information and analytical studies, including epidemiology and statistical analysis.*
b. A specialist responsible for the planning and co-ordination of child health and liaison with the local education authority.
c. A small number of specialists responsible for (i) psychiatric services and liaison with the personal social services department on mental health problems; (ii) geriatric services and services to the chronic sick and disabled, and liaison with the local authority in relation to these services and (iii) co-ordination of the development of health centres.

* This officer may also have responsibilities in relation to environmental health.

75

4.34.　He will also usually have on his staff a health education officer, a chief chiropodist and a chief speech therapist, all of whom will be accountable to him for deployment and performance within their own fields.

4.35.　The AMO will be accountable to the AHA for functions delegated to him. He will not be accountable for District performance but will share monitoring and co-ordinating authority in relation to the DMTs and co-ordinating authority in relation to the Area Dental Officer and Area Pharmaceutical Officer, both of whom will, as heads of their professions, be directly appointed by the AHA. He may also co-ordinate some paramedical services. In addition he will be accountable directly to the local authority for those functions which he exercises on its behalf, e.g. to the education authority for its part of the school health service. Should he assign any of these functions to the DCP, he will remain responsible for the latter's performance in this limited sphere. Finally, the AMO will be regarded as the professional head in the Area of the specialty of community medicine and will co-ordinate the community medicine team throughout the Area. In an AHA(T) he will have the benefit of working closely with the professional staff of the department of social or community medicine of the medical school.

Regional Medical Officer

4.36.　The Regional Medical Officer (RMO) will be a member of the Regional Team of Officers. In this capacity, he shares responsibility for advising the RHA, establishing guidelines for AHA planning, reviewing and challenging Area plans and monitoring the performance of Area Teams of Officers. He will have particular responsibilities for the Regional planning of operational health-care services. Specifically he will:

a. *Co-ordinate the development of planning guidelines* for AHAs on Regional policies and priorities for the operational health-care services. The guidelines will often be developed by multi-disciplinary service-planning teams, specialising in particular health-care groups.
b. *Develop priorities for the distribution of medical specialties*, the deployment of medical manpower and the scheduling of capital project starts.
c. *Review AHA planning proposals* for operational health-care services, particularly in relation to the agreed guidelines.
d. *Co-ordinate the briefing stage* of capital building projects with a significant medical content.

4.37.　He will also have a number of individual responsibilities. He will, for example:

a. Ensure that the Regional medical advisory machinery can work effectively.
b. Provide the necessary personnel services for Regionally-employed medical staff.
c. Co-ordinate the development of postgraduate medical education and training throughout the Region, in liaison with the postgraduate dean.
d. Recommend priorities for the use of RHA funds available for health-care research, and co-ordinate community medicine research in liaison with the departments of social medicine and of general practice of the associated medical school and other universities.

e. Develop in conjunction with other disciplines adequate and effective health-care information systems throughout the Region.

4.38. The RMO will also monitor the extent and effectiveness of collaboration between the AHAs and the local authorities in relation to health-care planning.

4.39. The RMO will manage the Regional Pharmaceutical Officer and the Regional Scientific Officer and co-ordinate the work of the Director of the Regional Blood Transfusion Service. He will also have a number of specialists in community medicine accountable to him. The number will vary according to the size of population and other characteristics of the Region. These specialists will have functional responsibilities as follows:

a. *Health-care service planning and monitoring.* These medical officers will assist the RMO to co-ordinate the planning and monitoring activity, often supported by multi-disciplinary service-planning teams.

b. *Capital building projects.* This medical officer will co-ordinate the briefing stage of major capital building projects and give specialist medical advice to multi-disciplinary project teams.

c. *Information services and research.* This medical officer will be responsible for developing, introducing and maintaining effective health-care information systems throughout the Region.

d. *Personnel and postgraduate medical education.* This medical officer will be responsible for the administration* of contracts of Regionally-employed consultants and senior registrars and for liaison with the postgraduate dean and the postgraduate education committee. He will also be responsible for the general deployment of medical staff.

4.40. In addition to these functional responsibilities, each specialist in community medicine will also have expertise in subject areas e.g. psychiatric services, and will advise the service-planning teams in their particular spheres of interest.

4.41. The RMO will be accountable to the RHA for those functions delegated to him. AMOs will not be his subordinates and he will not be accountable for their performance, but, as a member of the Regional Team of Officers, he will share monitoring and co-ordinating authority over Area Teams of Officers.

CHAPTER 5

DENTISTRY

5.1. The dental profession is represented in all three existing arms of the NHS and in each case its position is now, and will continue to be, substantially similar to that of the medical profession. Reorganisation has therefore much the same implications for dentistry as it has for medicine:

a. Dental consultants and their subordinates will be employed by AHAs or RHAs under exactly the same conditions as medical consultants and their subordinates.

* He will work closely with the AMO of any AHA(T).

b. General dental practitioners will have a similar contractual relationship to their Family Practitioner Committees (FPCs) to that of general medical practitioners.

c. The contracts of dental officers now employed by local authorities will be transferred to the AHA, as will the contracts of local authority school medical officers, and they will be accountable to a dental officer of the AHA.

d. Dentists giving personal clinical services will contribute to management.

5.2. It follows therefore that many of the detailed arrangements proposed for doctors in the reorganised NHS will apply equally to dentists.

5.3. Nonetheless, apart from the perceived identity of the profession itself, dentistry has characteristics which distinguish it from medicine and so necessitate some organisational differences. In particular, there is relatively less hospital dental practice and general practice is more preponderant. In addition, general dental practitioners are less dependent than doctors on complementary health services, such as hospitals, home nursing, etc.

5.4. Thus, whilst co-operation between dental and other health services is necessary, there is not the same need for integration at the District level for dentistry as there is for medicine, and in general the organisational focus of dentistry will be at Area rather than District or Region. For this and other reasons, some special arrangements are required for dentistry, which are described in this Chapter.

Area

5.5. The AHA will be the central management point for dentistry:

a. providing directly the salaried school dental service, priority dental services etc.;

b. contracting with general dental practitioners, via the FPC;

c. holding contracts of specialists (except those held by the RHA viz., consultants and senior registrars working outside AHA(T)s).

5.6. There should be an Area Dental Officer (ADO) whose duties will include those of the present local authority Principal School Dental Officer:

a. planning and managing the school dental health services and the priority service for mothers and young children, in collaboration with the local authority and the medical officer responsible for school health, and managing the Area's auxiliary dental staff and dental laboratory service (if any);

b. providing dental advice to the local authority.

In addition, the role of the ADO will include:

c. providing dental advice to the AHA;

d. monitoring and seeking to co-ordinate the overall dental service provided to the Area, both by his own staff and by general dental practitioners and the hospital service;

e. preparing plans for improving the service and seeking the agreement of the independent clinicians to put them into practice;

f. liaison with the dental teaching hospital.

5.7. The ADO will not have powers of direction in clinical matters over the hospital or general dental practitioners in the Area. However, by reason of the special training he will receive, by his position as adviser to the AHA and by the knowledge and experience that he can acquire as an administrator in touch with the profession, he will be able to exercise an effective co-ordinating and guiding influence over the profession as a whole and thereby generally promote the improvement of the dental service in the Area.

5.8. In most Areas the ADO will be a full-time administrator. However, on the one hand, in some small Areas he may be able to combine clinical with his administrative duties whilst, on the other hand, in very large Areas he will need to be assisted by District Dental Officers with some administrative responsibility. He will invariably need appropriate clerical and administrative support.

5.9. Unlike the present Principal School Dental Officer, the ADO will be accountable directly to the Authority of and not to its medical officer. He will not be a member of the Area Team of Officers, since much of the team's work will not be of direct interest to him. However he will receive all team papers; he will attend meetings as of right whenever a matter to be discussed concerns or has implications for dentistry; he will have the right, on his own initiative, to propose matters concerning dentistry for discussion by the team and he will have the same right of access to the AHA as other members of the team and other chief professional officers. It will be for the AMO to co-ordinate the work of the ADO with the medical activities of the Area.

5.10. It should be the responsibility of the Area Administrator to ensure that appropriate matters arising in the Area Team of Officers are brought to the ADO's attention.

5.11. There will be an Area Dental Committee established as part of the AHA's statutory advisory machinery. The Committee will include representative general practitioner dentists, salaried dentists and hospital dental consultants, each of these elements being drawn from each District of a multi-District Area. The general practitioner element of the Committee could be provided from the members of the Local Representative Committee set up to advise the FPC on matters relating to contracts for general dental services. The Committee could communicate with the AHA and FPC either directly, or through the ADO, who would normally be invited to attend its meetings.

5.12. Dental consultants could participate in this and other advisory dental groups, without prejudice to their representation, through the relevant specialist divisions, on any medical advisory committees.

District

5.13. The school health service will be an Area responsibility, for which the AHA and the local authority will hold Area officers (the Area Medical, Dental and Nursing Officers) directly accountable. Subject, however, to approval as part of the AHA's plan for services, the ADO could nominate as District Dental Officers members of his staff who practise in the District, and might delegate some managerial responsibility to them. The District Dental Officer or ADO should have the same relationship to the DMT as the ADO to the Area Team of Officers. Unlike the full officer members of the DMT, however, the District Dental Officer will be directly accountable to the ADO, and the DMT will not normally be given discretion to alter priorities between the local school dental service and other services for which it is directly responsible.

5.14. In multi-District Areas there would be District Dental Committees which, as well as nominating members to the Area Dental Committee, would be able to nominate one dentist on to the District Medical Committee (general dental practitioner section), thus establishing local links between the two sides of general practice and providing the possibility that a general dental practitioner might be nominated on to the DMT (as could a dental consultant, via the hospital representative system).

Region

5.15. The RHA will exercise only a limited degree of decision making about dentistry, in the sense that it will mainly be interested in longer-term planning, including postgraduate education, and it should not need a full time Dental Officer. The RHA itself will receive advice from the professional advisory machinery and its officers and, in judging AHA's dental plans and monitoring their performance, might call on the Area Dental Officers as a group, or one selected from their number, to perform additionally as Regional Dental Officer.

CHAPTER 6
PHARMACY

6.1. The aim of the arrangements is to provide for:
a. organisation of managed pharmaceutical services on the scale recommended in the Noel Hall Working Party's Report on the hospital pharmaceutical service;
b. co-ordinated working of general practitioner pharmacists (chemist contractors in contract with the FPC and their pharmacist employees) with the managed services (pharmacists employed by the Health Authorities).

Area

6.2. Most Areas will be large enough to have their own organisation for hospital pharmaceutical services according to the Noel Hall recommendations (at least 8 pharmacists serving a minimum of about 2,500 beds and normally 4,000–6,000 beds). Areas smaller than this will need to use the organisation of a neighbouring AHA, which will attach the necessary pharmaceutical staff.

6.3. In an Area large enough to have its own organisation for managed services, the pharmaceutical staff will be managed by an Area Pharmaceutical Officer (APO), appointed by and accountable to the AHA. Pharmaceutical services for the Area, and any neighbouring Area for which the AHA provides a service, will be provided through departments managed by Principal and Staff Pharmacists. These will be accountable to the APO, some working at headquarters, others outposted to outlying hospitals.

80

6.4.   In an Area which is divided into Districts, but is not larger than the normal range referred to in paragraph 6.2 (6,000 beds), in each District the senior of the pharmacists will be designated as Pharmaceutical Officer. He will assist the APO to co-ordinate the services for the District and will have co-ordinating authority over, but will not be the manager of, the other heads of pharmaceutical departments outposted to the District.

6.5.   In an Area larger than the normal range referred to in paragraph 6.2 above (over 6,000 beds) and divided into Districts, in each District with 8 or more pharmacists a pharmacist will be appointed as District Pharmaceutical Officer. He will be accountable to the APO for the management of the pharmaceutical services of the District.

6.6.   The APO will therefore be responsible to his AHA, and to the AHA of any other Area for which he provides staff, for all the managed pharmaceutical services, including local manufacture and quality control and deployment of staff to maintain hospital dispensing facilities. His work will be co-ordinated with medical activities by the Area Medical Officer. The APO will receive agendas and papers for meetings of the Area Team of Officers and attend meetings when pharmaceutical matters are to be discussed. He will have right of access to the AHA and its Chairman.

6.7.   The APO could also act as the convenor of an Area Pharmaceutical Committee, established as part of the AHA's advisory machinery. The Committee would include representative general practitioner pharmacists (chemist contractors) and hospital pharmacists, both elements being drawn from each District of a multi-District Area. The general practitioner element of the Committee could be provided from the members of the Local Representative Committees set up to advise the FPC on matters relating to contracts for pharmaceutical services.

6.8.   In each District the Pharmaceutical Officer or District Pharmaceutical Officer will work closely with the District Medical Committee in measures for achieving economy in use of medicines and providing pharmaceutical advice to medical staff, and with the District Nursing Officer in systems of medicine administration and control of dangerous drugs. The work of the Pharmaceutical Officer or District Pharmaceutical Officer will be co-ordinated by the District Administrator on behalf of the DMT, either directly or through the Support Services Manager.

Region

6.9.   There must be machinery for the planning and co-ordination of pharmaceutical services in the Region, including:
a. recruitment, training and deployment of skilled personnel;
b. specification of suppliers and quality control;
c. location of manufacturing of items best manufactured on a Regional basis.

6.10.   A Regional Pharmaceutical Officer (RPO) will be appointed by and accountable to the Regional Medical Officer. In Regions with few AHAs, this could be a part-time post held by one of the APOs. The RPO will receive agendas and papers for meetings of the Regional Team of Officers and will attend meetings when pharmaceutical services are to be discussed. He will have right of access to the RHA and its Chairman.

6.11.   A suitably-constituted Regional Pharmaceutical Committee, established as part of the RHA's professional advisory machinery, could also assist in these planning and co-ordinating functions. It would include hospital and general practitioner pharmacists from each Area. It could be convened by the RPO.

CHAPTER 7
PARAMEDICAL WORK

7.1.   This Chapter deals with the arrangements needed to promote the co-ordinated working of paramedical staff. It excludes consideration of pharmacists, who are dealt with separately, and the great majority of opticians, who will work in contract with the FPC. Broadly, paramedical staff is taken to include all those, other than doctors, dentists and nurses, who are directly concerned with diagnosis or treatment in individual cases. These staff fall into two categories:
   a. scientific and technical staff covered by the Zuckerman Report who are concerned mainly with screening and diagnostic work;
   b. others whose work includes an element of direct therapy.

7.2.   The paramedical services have been organised mainly in very small sections and departments within the hospital service and, in some few cases, within the local authority health services. Most of these services, however, will be organised on a District basis, to be available both within hospitals and to medical practice outside hospitals, and implementation of the Zuckerman Committee's recommendations will result in larger consolidated departments of scientific and technical staff. The services might be situated geographically within hospitals or elsewhere.

A. SCIENTIFIC AND TECHNICAL SERVICES

District

7.3.   In accordance with the proposals in the Zuckerman Report, which are now beginning to be implemented nationally, scientific and technical staff at District level will be grouped into a small number of District-wide divisions. This grouping will be such as to bring together staff of related disciplines in which interchange is possible. Where a divisional grouping of staff creates a very large division, it may be sub-divided into departments.

7.4.   The AHA will appoint a consultant or a graduate scientist to be head of and managerially accountable for the scientists and technicians in each division and each department* that is established.

Where a division is organised in departments, one of the department heads

---

* These departments may contain consultants: they will be colleagues of the head of department who will co-ordinate their work.

will be designated as co-ordinator of the others so that the division may function effectively as a whole. These appointments as heads of divisions and departments will be made by the AHA, and the heads of divisions and departments will have access to the District Management Team. They will be monitored and where necessary co-ordinated by the District Administrator and will be monitored by consultants and GPs, prescribing the service for their patients, for the quality of service provided. As part of their monitoring activity the DMT will carry out a systematic review of all scientific and technical services.

7.5.   An example of a satisfactory grouping of scientific and technical staff follows. Other similar combinations might be equally satisfactory, depending upon the particular circumstances of the District and the services it provides.
   a. Pathology division, organised into four or five departments:
      —histopathology department: consultant histopathologist or morbid anatomist as head, with histopathology technicians and mortuary technicians;
      —medical microbiology department: consultant or graduate microbiologist or bacteriologist as head, with microbiology technicians;
      —haematology department: consultant or graduate haematologist as head, with haematology technicians;
      —chemical pathology department: consultant chemical pathologist or graduate biochemist as head, with pathology and biochemistry technicians;
      —clinical immunology: consultant clinical immunologist or graduate immunologist as head, with microbiology technicians.
   b. Clinical science division, organised in two departments, for example:
      —radiology department: consultant radiologist or radiotherapist as head, with scientific staff and radiographers (diagnostic and therapeutic);
      —clinical measurement department: consultant in cardiology, nuclear medicine or neurology as head, with scientific staff and audiology and EEG technicians.
   c. Physics Division: might have graduate physicist or bio-engineer as head and include electronic and physics technicians, bio-engineers, computer operators and programmers, dental technicians and surgical appliance technicians.

7.6.   Having a central District division or department for these groups of scientific and technical staff will not preclude their being individually attached, seconded or outposted to medical departments, health centres and clinics, or to consultants or GPs. In such cases the divisional or departmental head will remain professionally accountable for their work and the members will continue for career purposes to be members of the parent division or department. Examples might be:
   —an audiology technician attached to an ENT consultant or school medical officer.
   —ECG technicians outposted or seconded to a consultant cardiologist in a cardiology department.

7.7.   The senior graduate scientists will participate in the work of the appropriate divisions of the DMC and might be eligible for appointment to the Area Medical Advisory Committee.

Area

7.8.   One of the District scientific staff may be appointed by the AHA as Area convenor for each discipline. The Area convenor will negotiate temporary inter-District loans of personnel, where necessary, to cope with serious local shortages due to holidays, illness, etc.

Region

7.9.   There will be a Regional Scientific Officer, accountable to the Regional Medical Officer. He will formulate plans for the development of the scientific services within the Region and will co-ordinate the implementation of plans when adopted. He will also co-ordinate the recruitment, training and deployment of scientific and technical staff throughout the Region. He will act as convenor of a Regional Scientific Committee which will be established as part of the RHA's advisory machinery.

B. PARAMEDICAL THERAPY SERVICES

7.10.   The paramedical therapy services will similarly be organised on a District basis, and it may also be possible to group some staff with related skills in departments, each with its own head, on the lines indicated for scientific and technical staff in paragraphs 7.3 and 7.4.

7.11.   Subject to the possibility of adopting the foregoing kind of arrangement, the following shows the organisation envisaged in each District for the non-medically qualified professional and technical workers in each paramedical therapy service and, where attachment to clinics seems possible, the envisaged clinic.

art therapy: accountable to a consultant psychiatrist.

chiropody: accountable to a medical administrator.

clinical psychology: clinical psychologist may be a direct appointee of the AHA or accountable to a consultant psychiatrist.

dental work: auxiliaries, hygienists and surgery assistants accountable to a dental officer or consultant.

dietetics: accountable to a consultant in therapeutics or consultant physician; or may be direct appointee of the AHA.

industrial therapy: accountable to an administrator.

medical illustration: accountable to an administrator or a consultant in medical illustration.

music therapy: accountable to a consultant psychiatrist.

occupational therapy: accountable to a consultant in physical medicine, or may be a direct appointee of the AHA. May be attached or seconded to other specialties.

optical dispensing: accountable to consultant ophthalmologist, or may be a direct appointee of the AHA.

orthoptic therapy: accountable to consultant ophthalmologist.

physiotherapy: accountable to a consultant in physical medicine, or may be a direct appointee of the AHA. May be attached or seconded to other specialties.

psychotherapy:	psychotherapist may be a direct appointee of the AHA, or accountable to a consultant psychiatrist.
remedial gymnastics:	accountable to a consultant in physical medicine.
speech therapy:	accountable to a medical administrator or consultant psychiatrist, or ENT consultant.

7.12.   Where there is a consultant head of department, managerially accountable, the AHA may in addition appoint the senior member of the professional group (for example, a superintendent physiotherapist) as professional head of the department. This professional head will be accountable for ensuring that professional standards, as laid down by the Board of that profession, are maintained, and where appropriate, for assisting the consultant head of department to advise the DMT.

7.13.   Where the professional head of department is also head of a training school recognised (and therefore subject to inspection) by the Board of the relevant profession supplementary to medicine, the head might be accountable to the AHA for the management of the training school.

7.14.   Department heads will be monitored. In the case of AHA direct appointees, as for consultants in charge of paramedical departments, the department head will be monitored, and where necessary co-ordinated, by the district administrator, and will be monitored by the consultants and GPs prescribing the service for their patients on quality of service provided. As part of the monitoring service the DMT will carry out a systematic annual review of all the paramedical services.

Area

7.15.   One of the District professional heads for each paramedical discipline may be appointed by the AHA as Area convenor. The Area convenor will monitor services to ensure that professional and technical standards are being maintained, and will negotiate temporary inter-District loans of personnel where necessary to cope with serious local shortages due to holidays, illness, etc.

7.16.   If responsibility for the employment of social workers at present working in hospitals is transferred to the local authority social service departments, then details of the arrangements under which they will work for the new Health Authorities and take their place in the organisation, like other paramedical staff, will be the subject of negotiation.

7.17.   Chaplaincy services are conveniently considered under the head of paramedical work. They will be direct appointees of the AHA and the arrangements described for the appointment of a convenor for the Area and for monitoring within Districts can apply, so far as they are applicable.

Region

7.18.   It will be part of the Regional personnel function to plan and co-ordinate the recruitment, training and deployment of paramedical therapy staff within the Region.

85

CHAPTER 8
NURSING

8.1.   The Salmon and Mayston reports have given the nursing profession the opportunity to scrutinise its management of the nursing services and the personnel and training arrangements required. Implementation of the recommendations and the evident progress already made in these fields, has allowed the management study to consider only the organisational principles required for nursing in respect of NHS reorganisation. In effect, below the chief officer level within Districts, the reorganisation of nursing management will take the form of a fusion of the Salmon and Mayston structures. A brief indication of how this might be achieved, though allowing for considerable local flexibility, is set out in paragraph 8.5 below. This Chapter concentrates therefore on the principal responsibilities and tasks of the senior nurse at each level in the reorganised Service, and on the relationships between these nurses and the respective Authorities and Teams of Officers and between each other.

8.2.   The aim of these recommended arrangements for nursing is to provide for integrated community and hospital nursing services within Districts and co-ordination with other disciplines at each level of management. They are also intended to facilitate the provision of nursing advice and services required by local authorities in the exercise of their statutory functions e.g. in education and personal social services, and (subject to decisions to be taken in the light of the report of the Committee on Nursing (Chairman, Professor Asa Briggs)) to provide an organisation suited for nurse education purposes.

8.3.   The structure and function of nursing and midwifery professional advisory machinery did not directly concern the management study. The details of a possible pattern for the development and composition of such advisory machinery will need to be devised in consultation with the nursing and midwifery professions. RHAs and AHAs will have responsibility for establishing the machinery recommended, and the Regional and Area Nursing Officers the responsibility for ensuring balanced representation and its effective operation.

District

8.4.   In each District the nursing service will be managed by a District Nursing Officer (DNO), who will be a member of the District Management Team (DMT) and directly accountable to the AHA. The DNO will have a functional co-ordinating responsibility within the DMT and play a full role in the team's achievement of its objectives.

8.5.   Under the DNO the nursing service will be organised in "divisions", each under a divisional nursing officer. Proposed different ways of forming divisions are:
  a. A community nursing division and one or more hospital nursing divisions. There would be separate heads of the community and hospital nursing services, accountable to the DNO.
  b. Functional nursing divisions aligned, to some extent, with "health-care groups" e.g. a midwifery division, a psychiatry division, a general nursing division and a community care division. Each division would be managed

EXHIBIT XI

POSSIBLE NURSING ORGANISATIONAL
STRUCTURES WITHIN DISTRICTS

A. HOSPITAL AND COMMUNITY
   NURSING DIVISIONS

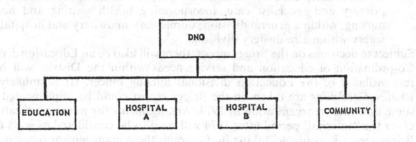

B. FUNCTIONAL DIVISIONS WITH A
   COMMUNITY CARE DIVISION

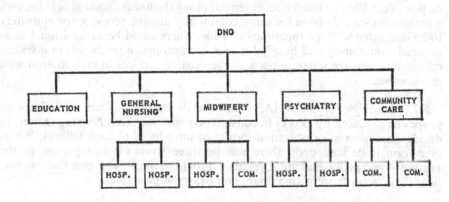

C. FUNCTIONAL DIVISIONS

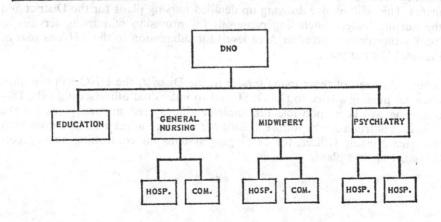

87

by a divisional nursing officer accountable to the DNO. The community care division would include either all community nurses, or health visitors only. In the latter case the divisional nursing officer would be responsible for advising the DNO on preventive nursing, health education and the nursing aspects of the school health service.

c. Functional nursing divisions, within which the various nursing services would be integrated for management purposes at an appropriate level e.g. primary and specialist care, incorporating health visiting and hospital nursing, within a general division; domiciliary midwifery and hospital midwifery within a midwifery division.

Subject to decisions on the Briggs report, there will also be an Education division. Co-ordination of education and service needs within the District will be the responsibility of the Education divisional nursing officer. (It is unlikely that whatever decisions are taken on the Briggs report could be implemented until some time after reorganisation in 1974. Arrangements for nursing education to cover the "interim" period after 1974 will need to be considered as soon as the Briggs report is available, taking into account these management recommendations.)

8.6.   There might be a phased progression from the arrangement described in sub-paragraph a. to those in sub-paragraphs b. and c. of paragraph 8.5 above depending upon the organisational situation at the time of reorganisation. Arrangements might be adopted for different skills within nursing e.g. it might be possible, within an overall arrangement along the lines suggested in b. i.e. with a community-care division for other community nursing services, for midwifery to be integrated within a functional division. There could be a transitional stage at which community and hospital nurses at appropriate levels within divisions continue to manage separate parts of the existing services in consultation with one another.

8.7.   It will be for the AHA, as advised by the Area Team of Officers on proposals produced by DMTs in consultation with the Area Nursing Officer, to decide what form of organisation should be introduced in each District. Whatever form is decided upon there will be three levels of management in the District; top-"policy-making"; middle-"programming"; and first-line-"operational", in accordance with Salmon and Mayston principles.

8.8.   As a member of the DMT, the DNO will be responsible for assessing the nursing needs of the District, in the light of service and educational requirements. This will involve drawing up detailed nursing plans for the District and the nursing budget (including proposals for provision of nursing services to local authorities as agreed at Area level) for submission to the AHA as part of the total District plan.

8.9.   As head of the nursing service in the District, the DNO will give professional nursing advice to the DMT and to individual officers within the District. She will be responsible for implementing agreed nursing plans for the District, controlling expenditure against the nursing budget and, in liaison with the Area Nursing Officer, for developing systems for controlling nursing performance against plans.

8.10.   The DNO will manage nursing staff within the District and will maintain professional standards of care to people both in the community and in hospital. She will control the operational activities of any Area nursing staff attached to District and co-ordinate the activities of any Area nursing staff outposted to District.

8.11.   It will be the responsibility of the DNO to ensure that nursing is co-ordinated with other activities within the District, through the participation of nurses as appropriate in multi-disciplinary team working at all levels. This will include membership of health-care planning teams. In each sector of the District, nurses will be designated for purposes of liaison with the administration and other skill groups. This responsibility will be carried in addition to normal management responsibilities. It will be necessary for the DNO to ensure that the implications of established policies and agreed plans are understood by nurses at all levels.

8.12.   On the DNO's staff and accountable to her will be a senior nurse who will work with the District Community Physician on school health questions. She will be the point of contact on day-to-day matters for head teachers, and arrange for the availability of nurses for school health services in clinics and in schools, as agreed at Area level and incorporated in District plans.

8.13.   In a multi-District Area, the work of the DNOs, both as members of the DMTs and as heads of the nursing service in the Districts, will be monitored and co-ordinated by the Area Nursing Officer.

8.14.   In an Area not divided into Districts the duties of DNO will be performed by the Area Nursing Officer, with the necessary staff to support her in both roles.

Area

8.15.   There will be an Area Nursing Officer (ANO), who will be a member of the Area Team of Officers and accountable to the AHA as the head of her profession in the Area, for providing professional nursing advice to the AHA, to the Area Team of Officers, to individual officers at the Area level and, as required, to the matching local authority. The ANO will have functional co-ordinating responsibility within the Area Team of Officers and play a full role in the Team's achievement of its objectives. Within the context of the Area Team of Officers' review of District proposals she will advise the AHA on the District plans in relation to their implications for nursing and on their nursing content. She will monitor and co-ordinate the performance of DNOs against established policies and agreed plans and advise the AHA of any action required.

8.16.   The ANO will co-ordinate nursing functions, including planning, with other functions at Area level and will participate in the joint consultative process between the AHA and the matching local authority. A senior nurse on her staff will have special advisory and co-ordinating responsibilities for child health, including the school nursing service e.g. the nursing aspects of the assessment of the needs of handicapped children. She will appoint and second nursing staff for service with the matching local authority for work for which the local authority has statutory responsibility e.g. the provision of residential accom-

89

modation for the elderly and the mentally handicapped. These nursing staff will remain professionally accountable to her. She will support DNOs in identifying the nursing service needs of their Districts, in drawing up detailed District nursing policies and plans and in implementing agreed plans. She will provide "client" advice to the Area works department on capital works delegated to Area level.

8.17.   The ANO will promote plans for nursing research and studies and take part in the evaluation of such plans within the Regional programme. She will be responsible for assessing the requirements for nurse training and the professional development of staff throughout the Area and for arranging with DNOs that the necessary provision is made in District plans to provide for an effective nursing service in line with statutory requirements for nurse education. She will also ensure the effective operation of professional nursing and midwifery advisory machinery.

8.18.   The ANO will need staff to assist her to carry out certain of her functions e.g. personnel and training, and school health services.

Region

8.19.   There will be a Regional Nursing Officer (RNO), who will be a member of the Regional Team of Officers and directly accountable to the RHA. The RNO will have functional co-ordinating responsibility within the team and play a full role in the team's achievement of its objectives. She will have responsibilities respectively as the head of her profession in the Region, as a member of the Regional Team of Officers and as manager of nursing staff at Regional level.

8.20.   The RNO will provide professional nursing advice to the RHA and to other officers at Regional level, including the briefing and planning concerned with capital building.

8.21.   The RNO will ensure that ANOs are informed of national and Regional nursing policies, and will contribute to the formulation of national policies by reflecting the views of the profession in the Region to the Department.

8.22.   As a member of the Regional Team of Officers, the RNO will advise on the adequacy of the nursing content of proposed Area plans, and on the development and review of policies for AHA planning and the challenging of District plans. She will monitor and co-ordinate the work of ANOs against established policies and agreed plans and advise the RHA on any action which might be necessary. She will also ensure the co-ordination of nursing with other activities at Regional level and, in conjunction with other disciplines, will participate in the development of and the use of health-care information systems in the Region.

8.23.   The RNO will co-ordinate the development of post-certificate nursing education and training in the Region. She will be responsible for planning programmes of nursing research through liaison with Universities and other educational establishments. She will identify the management training needs of senior nursing staff in the Region and secure the provision of training facilities. She will also provide the nursing content for other training programmes.

8.24.   The RNO will ensure the effectiveness of collaboration on nursing

90

matters between local authorities and AHAs, and the effective operation of professional nursing and midwifery advisory machinery in the Region.

8.25. The RNO will need subordinate staff to assist her, and in particular to carry out her personnel and training functions and to serve on service-planning and capital building project teams.

CHAPTER 9

WORKS

9.1. This chapter describes the proposed organisation of new Health Service building, building and engineering maintenance and operations, and property management at Region, Area and District.

A. RESPONSIBILITIES: ALLOCATION BETWEEN LEVELS

(1) New building

9.2. The Department will continue to carry out its present functions in respect of new building works. Delegation to RHAs will be based not primarily on works cost, but on building type. Thus the Department will concern itself primarily with those projects which display special features of type or design of major significance for service development.

9.3. In respect of these selected ("starred") projects only, RHAs will be required to obtain DHSS approval for strategic planning, and subsequently only for such of the planning design process as is necessary in relation to each particular project.

9.4. Extending this principle of delegation the RHA will, at its discretion, delegate responsibility to the AHA, subject to such conditions as Region considers it necessary to impose, and provide the AHA with the necessary capital finance for the achievement of named projects selected from the following categories:
a. building types at present executed by local health authorities (health centres, ambulance stations, clinics etc.);
b. residential accommodation;
c. administrative accommodation (offices, stores, etc.);
d. works at existing hospitals involving the addition, upgrading or extension of single departments or simple complexes of departments;
provided that the contemplated works are adequately covered by guidance material, that the site development implications are acceptable to the RHA and that the work does not form part of a phased reconstruction programme being executed by the RHA.

9.5. The RHA will also provide the AHA with a block of capital for other minor capital works (e.g. improvement or replacement), in accordance with guidance by the RHA.

91

(2) Maintenance

9.6. For the purposes of this paper, "maintenance" is defined as "the building and engineering work needed to keep buildings, plant and equipment operationally efficient for current use". It does not include work needed to rectify design or specification defects occurring in a new building within, say, two years after it has been brought into use, nor any but minor upgrading or change of use or plant replacement. The cost of such works should be properly regarded as capital expenditure. The maintenance work involved falls into three main types:

 a. Execution of programmed and running maintenance for plant, fabric, building services and grounds.

 b. Engineering and equipment operation at institutional level.

 c. Specialist maintenance, e.g. electronic, bio-medical, fire prevention and X-ray equipment, lifts, laundries etc.

9.7. The following allocation of maintenance responsibilities between levels is proposed:

 a. The Department to provide policy guidance on building and engineering maintenance and a framework for reviewing performance, and to make available to the field authorities the necessary professional and technical leadership, guidance and support.

 b. The RHA to be responsible for providing the AHA with professional guidance in line with national policy; providing some highly specialised technical expertise on aspects of maintenance; approving maintenance programmes of the AHA; ensuring feed-back to designers and reviewing, by physical inspection or other means, the maintenance performance of AHAs.

 c. The AHA to be responsible for formulating, within national and Regional policy guidance, maintenance programmes, which would originate at unit and District levels, for execution of maintenance within its Districts; for providing maintenance staff; for arranging maintenance contracts with local authorities or other agencies and for monitoring the implementation of the maintenance programme.

(3) Property management

9.8. The term "property management" is used to describe the management functions relating to land and property transactions and estate development (i.e. the economic use of property assets). It does not include the land survey function.

9.9. The following allocation of property management functions between levels is proposed:

 a. The Department to be responsible for issuing policy guidance on property acquisition and disposal; for maintaining central records (e.g. the National Terrier); for providing finance for acquisitions; for compulsory purchase orders and for approval of Regional proposals falling outside prescribed limits of delegation.

 b. The RHA to be responsible for conducting all acquisitions and disposals not reserved to the Department; for all consultations with other estate owners; for consultation with local authority valuers at Regional level and with the Regional Office of the Property Services Agency of the Department of the Environment; for the control of finance for property transactions; for the maintenance of Terriers and other records of NHS property within the Region and for valuation, except where this is a prescribed function of the District Valuer.

c. The AHA to act as agent of Region in property transactions, in liaison both with local authorities (including their Valuers' Departments) and with other estate owners, and for the day-to-day administration of the NHS estate within the Area (e.g. tenancies, complaints).

B. PROPOSED ORGANISATION

9.10. The following paragraphs describe the necessary organisation at each level for each of the major functions.

(1) District

9.11. There will be a District Building Officer (DBO) and a District Engineer (DE) in each District. These officers will be:

a. accountable to the District Administrator for all activities financed from the District maintenance budget. Depending on the nature and extent of the workload, the District Administrator may depute the handling of day-to-day matters to the appropriate member of his senior staff. To provide a single point of contact, one of the two officers (DBO and DE) will be nominated to co-ordinate their activities;

b. accountable to their professional and technical heads at Area in relation to the professional and technical content of their work and for personnel matters.

(2) Area

9.12. The AHA will have some new building projects delegated by the RHA, other minor building works referred to in paragraph 9.5 and some property management functions, but the main concern of the works services at Area will be with building and engineering maintenance and operations and with commissioning new buildings, working within general guidance from Region.

9.13. The overall responsibility for the works functions will rest with an Area Works Officer (AWO). In larger Areas (defined by reference to the extent of delegated building works from Region and the complexity of maintenance delivered from Area, rather than within Districts), he will be directly accountable to the AHA. In this case, although not a full member of the Area Team of Officers, he will receive all agendas, papers and minutes and have the right to attend team meetings when matters which he considers critical to the works function are to be discussed.

9.14. The AWO will be responsible for:

a. Providing a single point of contact, on behalf of the works professions, with the user or client professions within the Area.

b. Progressing the design and construction of capital works delegated from the RHA, using design expertise from Region, outside consultants or the local authority when necessary. (See paragraph 20.)

93

c. Participating in the formulation of Area plans and budgets by formulating plans for Area works activity, ensuring that District plans contain satisfactory programmes and budgets for maintenance and ensuring that Area plans take account of implications for building and engineering.
d. Ensuring that the building and engineering work carried out at District is of a satisfactory professional and technical standard.
e. Supporting District works staff with specialist services for maintenance of e.g. X-ray, lifts and fire prevention equipment.
f. Providing personnel management for the works professionals and maintenance and operational staff in the Area, i.e. in training, career planning and development, deployment and advising on appointments.

9.15.   To assist him in the discharge of his functions, the AWO in the larger Areas will have two subordinates accountable to him:
a. an Area Building Officer
b. an Area Engineer.

9.16.   In smaller Areas, most of which will not be divided into Districts, the AWO function will be combined with that of the DBO or the DE.
a. In an Area not divided into Districts, either the DBO or the DE will be nominated to provide the advice to the Area Administrator or the Area Team of Officers necessary for them to discharge their Area functions.
b. In Areas that, although small, are divided into Districts, one of the DEs or one of the DBOs will be nominated.
In both cases, all officers will be monitored and co-ordinated by their Regional professional heads on technical and personnel matters.

9.17.   In some Areas it may be desirable to establish at Area level specialised staff technicians for work requiring specialist expertise (e.g. lifts, sterilisers, fuel monitoring). Such staff will be accountable to the AWO and outposted as necessary to Districts.

9.18.   The District maintenance budget will be prepared by the District Administrator and agreed by the DMT, on the basis of technical proposals for the programme of work provided by the DE and DBO. These proposals will be prepared with advice from the AWO and his staff, following policy guidelines set by the RHA (advised by the RWO) and by the AHA (advised by the AWO).
a. The budget will be approved first by the AHA, with the advice of the AWO, and then finally by the RHA with the advice of the RTO. Arrangements will be made as part of the budgetary process (see Chapter 3) to ensure that funds provided for maintenance purposes are not used for other purposes.
b. Adjustment of priorities within the programme of work will be made by the District Administrator in consultation with the DBO and DE. In the case of a dispute on technical grounds the AWO will also be consulted.

9.19.   AHA plans will contain a definition of capital building work required. The majority of this work will be delivered by the RHA. Some projects, however, will be delegated to the AHA for progressing from conception, through briefing and design, to construction, commissioning and evaluation. The responsibility for conducting this work, and the allocation of functions between professions and the Area multi-disciplinary project team for each stage and for the project as a whole, will be similar to that described later for Region.

9.20.   There will be no architect-led design capacity at Area level. The RWO will indicate to Area how design work is to be done, normally by one of the following four methods:

a. By the Area Building Officer or Engineer, when within his professional capability.
b. By the local authority architect, when the project forms part of a complex of mainly local authority buildings.
c. By Regional staff.
d. By consultant designers nominated by the Region.

9.21.   Area matters related to property management will be dealt with by a subordinate of the Area Administrator, with advice from Region.

(3) Region

9.22.   A Regional Works Officer (RWO) will be accountable for the design and construction of all the building and engineering works carried out by each Region. He will be a full member of the Regional Team of Officers and will be the manager of the Regional Architect, Engineer and Quantity Surveyor. He will be responsible for:

a. Providing a single point of contact at the highest level on behalf of the works professions with the user or client professions.
b. Participating fully in the Regional Team of Officers' preparation of planning guidelines, review of AHA plans and preparation of RHA plans.
c. Ensuring that the RHA and Regional Team of Officers are aware of the works implications of plans.
d. Delivering all capital works to match the requirements specified in the client's brief, including maintaining costs within budget.
e. Recommending to the RHA the new building works to be delegated to AHAs.
f. Maintaining a high professional and technical standard in building and engineering throughout the Region, including within each of its Areas, by monitoring and co-ordinating Area works staff.
g. Reviewing and approving the AHA maintenance budgets.

9.23.   The Regional Architect would have one new section reporting to him, that of a surveyor responsible for providing professional advice to the Regional Administrator on property management and on building maintenance policy and land survey.

9.24.   AHA and RHA plans will contain a definition of capital building works required. These will be translated into a capital building programme by the RHA. This translation will be done by a capital building programme committee, which will include a medical officer, a nurse, an administrator, a finance officer, the Regional Architect, Engineer and Quantity Surveyor. The medical or administrator member would normally be nominated Chairman by the RTO. The administrator member of this Committee will be the Region's Capital Development Officer responsible for co-ordination and administrative control of the capital building programme as a whole and accountable to the Regional Administrator.

95

9.25. Regional staff will be responsible for progressing each project not delegated to AHA from conception, through briefing and design, to construction. The "lead" responsibility for preparing the brief for each project, including maintaining estimated costs within budget, will rest with an administrator or a medical officer depending on the nature of the project. He will be supported and advised by a multi-disciplinary capital building project team, including medical, nursing, administrative, finance and works officers from Region and, where appropriate, from Area and District. Each project team will be co-ordinated by a project administrator, who will ensure that projects keep to programme by:

a. watching for delays and difficulties and identifying causes;
b. ensuring that project team members are made aware of them and their consequences;
c. suggesting ways of resolving the problems;
d. endeavouring to resolve them by personal exhortation in the first instance then, if necessary, by formal approach, through the Regional Administrator to the professional officers concerned.

9.26. The responsibility for design and construction and maintaining costs within budget during these stages will rest with the Regional Architect, the Regional Engineer or the Regional Quantity Surveyor, depending on the nature of the work, each accountable to the RWO.

9.27. The responsibility for initiating and guiding the commissioning will rest with the project administrator, but the executive work will be delegated to Area.

9.28. The responsibility for evaluation will rest with the capital building programme committee, working within guidance from DHSS.

CHAPTER 10
FINANCE

10.1. An important objective in the reorganised NHS is to place responsibility on management for the effective use of resources (manpower, materials, etc.). At the higher levels this will be achieved by planning, by setting objectives and by deciding on alternatives and priorities. At lower levels it will be achieved by using resources efficiently. The use of resources is ultimately expressed in terms of money, as a common measure. Managers at all levels should therefore understand and take account of the financial implications of their proposals and their actions.

10.2. Although all disciplines should be finance-conscious, the financial appraisal of proposals and action, and the provision of financial information for purposes of control requires the use of a separate expertise. Both AHAs and RHAs in the reorganised NHS will, therefore, require suitably qualified finance officers and staff for their finance departments. These staff will largely be drawn from the same sources as staff for the administrative function, but need special training. Finance officers will perform three main functions:

a. provide financial advice to the Authority, to its management, to its officer teams and to its officers individually;

b. provide financial services;

c. take part in and co-ordinate the preparation of budgets.

In addition, although all managers will be accountable for economy, efficiency and the effective use of resources, finance officers have a special but not exclusive responsibility for these matters. They are responsible for ensuring that all existing services or new proposals are subjected to critical financial appraisal with a view to achieving efficiency and value for money. At each level the finance officer will be a member of the officer team (Regional Team of Officers (RTO) Area Team of Officers (ATO) and District Management Team (DMT)), be accountable directly to the Authority and form part of a chain of responsibility extending from the Accounting Officer of the DHSS downwards through the Service.

10.3.   The financial services to be provided include:

a. accountancy and cashier services for expenditure (including salaries, wages and creditor payments) and for income due to the Authority, and preparation of statutory accounts;

b. organisation of financial control systems, supervision and internal audit;

c. compiling financial estimates for planning purposes and taking part in the preparation of budgets within financial allocations;

d. monitoring budgets and providing financial information to management at all levels, technical control of budgets and monitoring overall budget and cash positions and the use of reserves.

District

10.4.   A suitably qualified District Finance Officer (DFO) will be appointed for each District. He will be a member of the DMT, responsible for co-ordinating the preparation of budgets, for providing financial advice to the DMT, for monitoring adherence to budget by officers within the District, for monitoring performance to help ensure that value is obtained and waste avoided and for complying with financial policies set by the AHA and by higher Authorities. He will provide such financial services as may be required by the Area Treasurer and will be accountable to the AHA for ensuring that statutory financial regulations are adhered to in the District. The DFO's work will be monitored by the Area Treasurer, who will exercise co-ordinating authority in relation to all financial services provided by the DFO.

Area

10.5.   Each AHA will appoint a suitably qualified Area Treasurer (AT), who will be a member of the ATO. The AT will be responsible for consolidating District accounts in the preparation of Area accounts and for co-ordinating the preparation of Area budgets, including those built up from District budgeting processes. He will provide financial advice to the AHA and to the ATO and will monitor expenditure on direct Area services and ensure adherence to budget. He will ensure compliance by DFOs with the AHA's financial policies. The AT will attach finance staff to the FPC. These will be under the FPC Administrator's operational control, the AT retaining accountability for the effectiveness of the financial procedures and the accuracy of the accounts. The AT will also act as

97

professional head of the whole finance organisation and will be accountable for monitoring adherence to statutory financial regulations throughout the Area.

Region

10.6. Each RHA will appoint a suitably qualified Regional Treasurer (RT) to provide them with financial advice (e.g. in allocating finance to AHAs and reviewing their plans and budgets, in monitoring their expenditure and their use of resources and in making decisions on the RHA's own operations), and to be responsible for all financial services needed by the RHA for the purpose of its functions and for the preparation of the Regional budget and accounts.

10.7. The RT will have direct access to the RHA and will be the professional head of the finance organisation throughout the Region. He will monitor and, where necessary, co-ordinate the work of ATs to ensure that adequate budgets are developed and that Areas are functioning within the financial policies established by the RHA.

CHAPTER 11

ADMINISTRATION AND RELATED SKILLS

11.1. The effective management and administration of the NHS is a task requiring the skills of many different professions and covering a wide range of functions. The administrative roles of doctors, nurses and other health professions in the reorganised NHS have been described in previous Chapters, and the finance and works functions have also been covered. This Chapter describes the organisation required to carry out the following three responsibilities, which are the reason why administrators are employed in the NHS.

a. *Managing institutional and other support services.* These services include ambulance services, hotel services (catering, domestic, portering and laundry), CSSD, supplies, maintenance of medical records, personal transport and general oversight of property transaction—buying, selling, letting, handling complaints, etc. Running these services effectively is a major responsibility. Together they account for almost 20 per cent of the total health services' revenue expenditure (nearly £400 million a year).

b. *Providing administrative services.* Administrators will provide the Secretariat for RHAs and AHAs and the staff needed to enable FPCs and Community Health Councils to carry out their functions, and they will arrange for specialist advice and support to Authorities, professional staff and fellow administrators on personnel, management services, legal matters and relations with public and press. In addition, administrators will be responsible for accommodation and office services.

c. *Acting as general co-ordinators.* Hitherto hospital administrators have co-ordinated the activities of institutional and support services with each other and with those of professional staff providing care for patients in hospital, and Clerks to Executive Councils have fulfilled similar functions in respect of services provided by independent contractors. These functions will continue to be important to the effectiveness of the hospital and family practitioner services. However, the proposed reorganisation of the Health Service and of local government imposes further requirements for general co-ordination. Administrators will be equal members of multi-disciplinary teams at each level and, as such, will be responsible for the general administrative co-ordination of each of the teams. In addition, the introduction of a formal planning process requires the administrator to act as general co-ordinator for the formulation of support services plans, for the working of the total planning process and for the implementation of agreed plans.

11.2.   At each operating level in the reorganised Service there will be an administrator who will be accountable to his employing Authority for the institutional, support and administrative services deployed at his level, and for providing general co-ordination. Thus:

a. *At district level,* the District Administrator (DA) will act as general coordinator to the District Management Team (DMT). In addition, he will be accountable to the AHA for hotel services,* medical records,† stores and personal transport, and he will be responsible for office accommodation and services. The administrative organisation within Districts is shown in Exhibit XII. It will vary in detail, depending on the local situation, but the DA may need to be supported by:
—A Support Services Manager, accountable to the DA for hotel services, stores, personal transport and medical records in the District.
—A General Administrator, accountable for secretariat, accommodation and office services, administrative support to all staff involved in the planning process and for personnel services.
—Sector Administrator(s),‡ who will manage or co-ordinate the various institutional and operational support services in the health centres, clinics and hospitals and see that they combine effectively with doctors, nurses, paramedical and social services staff. Sector Administrators will be accountable either to the DA or to the Support Services Manager.
b. *At Area level,* the Area Administrator (AA) will be the Secretary to the AHA and will act as general co-ordinator to the Area Team of Officer (ATO). He will be accountable for the ambulance service, where this is provided by the AHA, for the Area supplies service and for any other institutional, support or administrative services provided from the Area, including property management. He will provide advice on personnel and management services for Area and District staff, and will be responsible for the administrative contribution to the planning process. He will also provide accommodation and office services for AHA staff. He will be the professional head of administrators throughout the Area. The proposed Area administrative organisation is shown in Exhibit XIII. It includes, directly subordinate to the AA, an Administrator (Family Practitioner Services) serving the FPC, a Personnel Officer, a Supplies Officer, and

* except where these are provided on an Area-wide basis, e.g. laundry.
† other than FPC records.
‡ "Sector" is used to describe levels of administrative management below the District, and Sector Administrators will be analogous to the present hospital secretaries. The sector is not a distinct management tier, in the sense that a District is.

EXHIBIT XII

DISTRICT ADMINISTRATIVE ORGANISATION

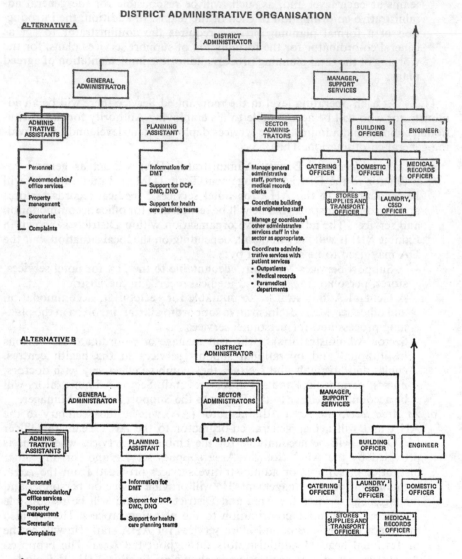

ALTERNATIVE A

DISTRICT ADMINISTRATOR

GENERAL ADMINISTRATOR

MANAGER, SUPPORT SERVICES

ADMINISTRATIVE ASSISTANTS
- Personnel
- Accommodation/ office services
- Property management
- Secretariat
- Complaints

PLANNING ASSISTANT
- Information for DMT
- Support for DCP, DMC, DNO
- Support for health care planning teams

SECTOR ADMINISTRATORS
- Manage general administrative staff, porters, medical records clerks
- Coordinate building and engineering staff
- Manage or coordinate[3] other administrative services staff in the sector as appropriate.
- Coordinate administrative services with patient services
  - Outpatients
  - Medical records
  - Paramedical departments

BUILDING OFFICER[2]

ENGINEER[2]

CATERING OFFICER[1]

DOMESTIC OFFICER[1]

MEDICAL RECORDS OFFICER[1]

STORES SUPPLIES AND TRANSPORT OFFICER[1]

LAUNDRY, CSSD OFFICER[1]

ALTERNATIVE B

DISTRICT ADMINISTRATOR

GENERAL ADMINISTRATOR

SECTOR ADMINISTRATORS

As in Alternative A

MANAGER, SUPPORT SERVICES

ADMINISTRATIVE ASSISTANTS
- Personnel
- Accommodation/ office services
- Property management
- Secretariat
- Complaints

PLANNING ASSISTANT
- Information for DMT
- Support for DCP, DMC, DNO
- Support for health care planning teams

BUILDING OFFICER

ENGINEER

CATERING OFFICER[1]

LAUNDRY, CSSD OFFICER[1]

DOMESTIC OFFICER[1]

STORES SUPPLIES AND TRANSPORT OFFICER[1]

MEDICAL RECORDS OFFICER[1]

3 — Sector administrator will manage sector staff in some of these functions while he will coordinate them in others; the arrangements will vary among functions and districts, depending on the local situations

2 — The Building Officer and the Engineer will be accountable to the DA for all activities financed from the district maintenance budget; the DA may depute the handling of day-to-day matters to the appropriate member of his senior staff; one of the two officers will be nominated to coordinate both their activities; they will also be accountable to their professional and technical heads at Area in relation to the professional and technical content of their work and for personnel matters

EXHIBIT XIII

AREA ADMINISTRATIVE ORGANISATION

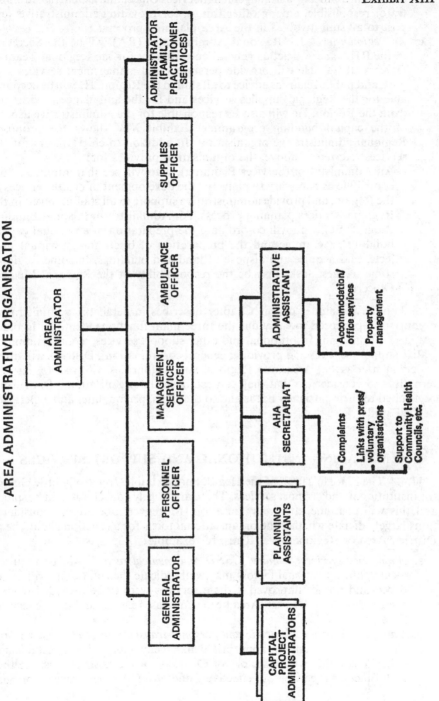

Ambulance Officer,* a Management Services Officer and a General Administrator responsible, among other things, for providing administrative support to all staff involved in the Area planning process.

c. *At Regional level*, the Regional Administrator (RA) will be the Secretary to the RHA and will act as general co-ordinator for the Regional Team of Officers (RTO). He will provide personnel and management services support, and public relations advice to all staff in the Region. He will be accountable for the Regional supplies services and for the ambulance services run from the Region. He will also be responsible for the administrative aspects of the capital building programme. Exhibit XIV shows the proposed Regional administrative organisation. In addition to chief officers for the services referred to above, the organisation provides for:

—An Administrator (Services Planning), who will see that administrators contribute as necessary to plans for the development of health services in the Region, and provide administrative support to all staff involved in the Regional services planning process. An Administrator (Capital Building Programme), who will co-ordinate the preparation of an annual capital building programme and the preparation of briefs for individual projects, and acquire and dispose of land and buildings. In some Regions, some of these tasks may be the responsibility of the Regional Medical Officer.

11.3.   The remainder of this Chapter describes in detail the administrative organisation proposed to carry out the three main functions identified in paragraph 11.1 (managing institutional and other support services, securing administrative support services and providing general co-ordination). Districts will differ widely in size, as will Areas and Regions, and Authorities will wish to have alternatives to consider, so that they can establish the organisational framework best suited to their particular needs and to the skills, personalities and experience of their staffs.

A. MANAGING INSTITUTIONAL AND SUPPORT SERVICES

11.4.   The reorganisation of the Health Service implies relatively little change for institutional and support services. These are largely concentrated in hospitals and this will continue after reorganisation. Moreover, operational considerations largely dictate whether the organisational focus for a function should be at District, Area or Regional level. Thus, for example:

a. *Ambulance services, laundry, CSSD and medical records* will be required locally, but operational factors may well indicate that unit costs will be reduced and service improved if these services were to be provided from a central base for a District, Area or in some cases e.g. the ambulance service, for a group of AHAs.

b. *Catering, portering, domestic and personal transport services* must be provided at unit level and the appropriate management organisation established either locally i.e. within sectors of Districts, or the District must see that each function is carried out effectively and ensure the necessary co-ordination.

* who will be referred to as "Chief Ambulance Officer".

EXHIBIT XIV

REGIONAL ADMINISTRATIVE ORGANISATION

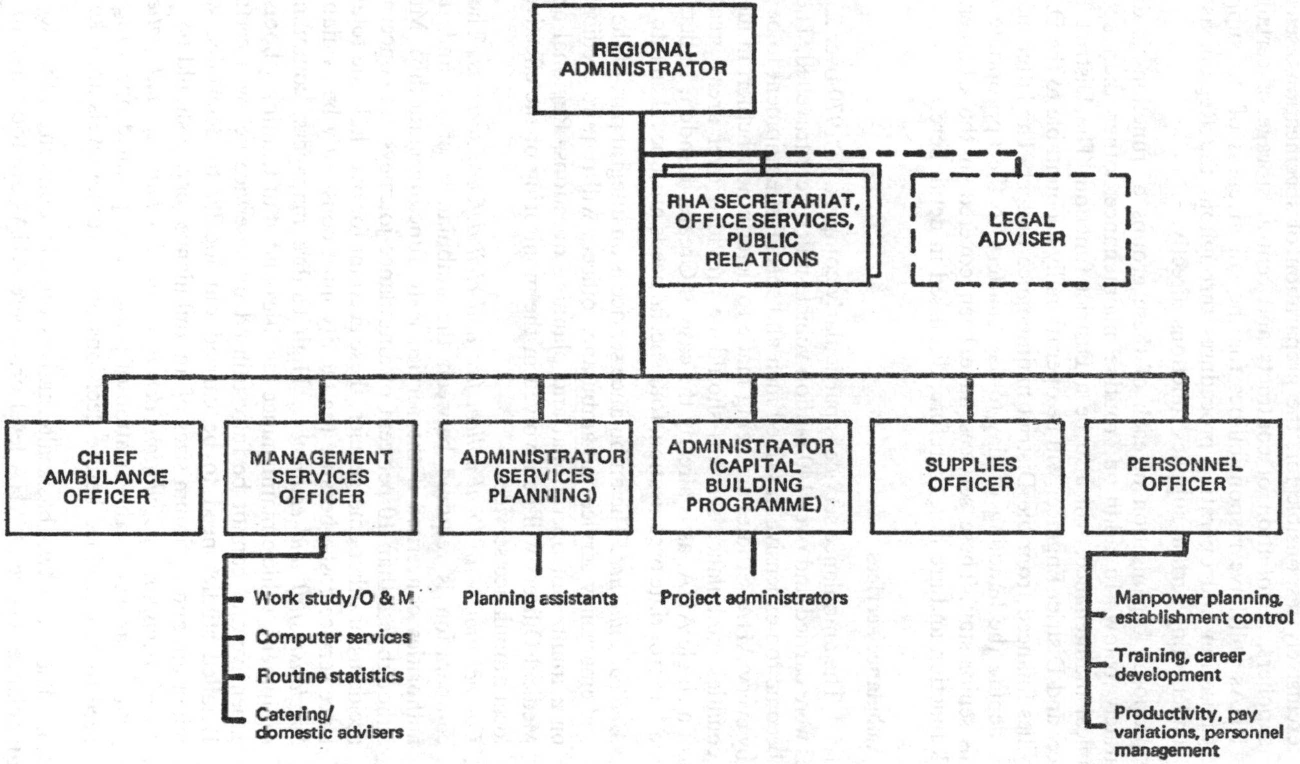

REGIONAL ADMINISTRATOR

RHA SECRETARIAT, OFFICE SERVICES, PUBLIC RELATIONS

LEGAL ADVISER

CHIEF AMBULANCE OFFICER

MANAGEMENT SERVICES OFFICER
- Work study/O & M
- Computer services
- Routine statistics
- Catering/domestic advisers

ADMINISTRATOR (SERVICES PLANNING)
- Planning assistants

ADMINISTRATOR (CAPITAL BUILDING PROGRAMME)
- Project administrators

SUPPLIES OFFICER

PERSONNEL OFFICER
- Manpower planning, establishment control
- Training, career development
- Productivity, pay variations, personnel management

Note: Posts of Administrator (Service Planning) and Administrator (Capital Building Programme) could be combined in smaller Regions

c. The supplies function will continue to involve staff at all levels in the service. District management will be largely responsible for storage, stock control and distribution of goods. Areas will be concerned with, but not exclusively responsible for, the preparation of specifications, selection of suppliers, negotiation of contracts and central storage of certain items. RHAs will have responsibilities for the effectiveness of the supplies organisation and operating procedures throughout the Region, as well as undertaking certain supplies functions directly.

The proposed organisation of each of these groups of functions is discussed separately below. In addition, routine maintenance, other than specialised technical maintenance, will also be a District function. The District Building Officer and District Engineer will be operationally accountable to the DA for all activities financed from the District maintenance budget. The latter may, however, depute the handling of day-to-day matters to the appropriate member of his senior staff. These services have been covered in the Chapter on the work function and are not, therefore, discussed in detail here.

(1) Ambulance services

11.5.   The ambulance service is particularly complex. In 1970 over 23 million cases were carried and over 140 million vehicle-miles were travelled. The service has become too expensive in skilled men and specialist equipment to be supported by every AHA. Studies are being made to determine whether, in metropolitan counties, ambulance services should be provided over areas greater than that of a single AHA, as is already the case in Greater London. In determining the most appropriate organisation, four special needs must be taken into account:

a. *Medical guidance.* The ambulance service is an integral part of the accident and emergency service and ambulance officers will require medical advice on a number of operational and planning questions. Regional and Area Medical Officers will be involved in the monitoring of the effectiveness of local ambulance services.

b. *Co-operation with local police, fire and civil defence services.* The closest co-operation is required between the ambulance service and the local authorities concerned if the service is to function smoothly. Moreover, although less than 10 per cent of ambulance journeys are concerned with accidents or other emergencies, these account for over half the total ambulance service costs, because the facility must constantly be available.

c. *Specialist staff and equipment.* High calibre managers, communications equipment, vehicle maintenance facilities and staff training schools, are all expensive and cannot be fully utilised by a service below a certain size. Detailed studies need to be carried out locally to determine what the minimum and optimum sizes of an ambulance service should be.

d. *Local transport, population density and distribution, and patient flow patterns,* as well as the location of present and planned operating centres, need to be examined before decisions on operating levels are taken.

11.6.   There are two basic alternatives outside London; either to provide an ambulance service at AHA level or, where AHAs are too small to support an effective service, to provide the ambulance service from the RHA. The organisational implications of the alternatives are as follows:

a. *Where the AHA provides the ambulance service* there will be a Chief Ambulance Officer, responsible to the AA, for the management and operational control of the Area ambulance service, and monitored by the Area Medical Officer on medical matters.

b. *Where the RHA provides the ambulance service*, e.g. in metropolitan areas outside London, there will be a Chief Ambulance Officer, employed by the RHA and accountable to the RA for the management and operational control of the services.

c. *At Regional level* there will be a Regional Ambulance Officer. He will be subordinate to the RA and will be monitored by the Regional Medical Officer. RHAs will need to consider whether the position of Regional Ambulance Officer could not be combined with that of Chief ambulance Officer for a multi-Area ambulance service.

In London (as mentioned in Chapter 2), special arrangements will need to be made for a "London Ambulance Service" to be transferred from the GLC to the NHS.

(2) Laundry and CSSD services

11.7. The organisation of these services will be comparatively unaffected by NHS reorganisation. Although the scope of their operations may well be substantially increased, one service should meet all local needs for clean linen and sterilised equipment. Thus, linen supplied for patients nursed at home and any special clothing, will come from the same service that meets hospital requirements. The internal organisation of these services will be similar to that for the catering, domestic and portering services:

a. *At the operating level*, which may be unit, sector, District or Area, depending on local conditions i.e. the extent of demand for the services, location of existing laundry and CSSD facilities, geographical distribution of units and ease of communication between them, there will be a laundry officer and a CSSD officer responsible for managing these services effectively, in compliance with agreed specification. These officers will be accountable either to Sector Administrators or to the Support Services Manager or to the AA, according to the circumstances and the pattern for administrative organisation which the AHA decides to adopt.

b. *At national level*, expertise, advice and guidance will be available on ways to improve the effectiveness or to reduce costs of laundry and CSSD services.

(3) Medical records

11.8. Medical records will be required at unit level, and the provision of an effective medical records service will be the responsibility of a District Medical Records Officer, accountable to the Support Services Manager. He will be responsible for the administration of all hospital records and for examining means of implementing policies for co-ordinating all medical records within the District. For example, he will look at ways of relating hospital records to FPC records.

(4) Catering, portering, domestic and personal transport services

11.9.   As stated above, little change to these services is implied by the re-organisation of the Health Service. The catering, portering and domestic requirements of the present local authority health services are small and can readily be met from hospital-based services. However, the effective management of these services will continue to be important not only to the welfare of patients, but also to the control of costs and the efficient use of resources. In 1970, these services cost over £160 million in England, 14 percent of total Health Service expenditure, and employed nearly 128,000 staff. The proposed organisation has the following main features:

   a. *At unit level (hospital or group of hospitals and associated health centres, clinics, etc)*, there will be a catering manager, domestic superintendent, head porter and general administrator (responsible for personal transport). These officers will be directly responsible for the service provided. They will be accountable for the performance of their staffs, either to a Sector Administrator or, in the case of catering and domestic staff, in some Districts to a functional head at District level.

   b. *At District level* there will be a District catering officer and District domestic service officer responsible for taking the lead on technical matters e.g. evaluating new techniques for improving services. In a small District, technical and management responsibilities at unit or sector level might be combined. In larger Districts and Areas not divided into Districts, Authorities may wish to establish separate posts.

   c. *At Area and Regional level*, catering and domestic officers subordinate to the Administrator, will provide technical support to their colleagues working in Districts and will be an independent source of advice to Authorities and their officers. They will review and agree proposals affecting catering or domestic services before these are incorporated in Authorities' plans. In addition, some large Areas, particularly in the bigger Regions, may require their own catering or domestic officers, but it will not be possible to determine the extent of this need until after the organisation described above has been in operation for 2–3 years.

(5) Supplies services

11.10.   The NHS procures over £200 million of goods and services every year. The supplies function i.e. preparing specifications, selecting potential suppliers, negotiating terms, placing orders for goods and arranging storage and distribution,* will involve all levels of the service:

   a. *At District level*, estimates of supply requirements will be prepared (and in some cases prices negotiated), goods will be ordered, received into stock and distributed to users. In addition, staff at District level will be responsible, within RHA and AHA supplies policies, for stock control and disposal of condemned, waste or surplus material. They will also need to provide facilities for and assistance in field trials and experiments to assess

---

* Movement of goods, i.e. bulk transport, will be a supplies function.

the value of new products and procedures. These functions will be the responsibility of an administrative officer accountable to the Support Services Manager.

b. *Area supplies staff* will prepare specifications for "common user" items i.e. items required by all units in the Area. Where national or Regional contracts are inappropriate they will select suppliers to be invited to quote and negotiate terms of supply. In some cases, Area supplies staff will themselves place orders for items for the Area as a whole and store and distribute these from central stores. Area staff will also advise District stores staff on stock control, storage and distribution problems. The Area supply function will be the responsibility of an Area Supplies Officer accountable to the AA. AHAs will need to consider the support staff needed. Two, perhaps three, assistant supplies officers will probably be required. The allocation of responsibilities between them will depend on their skills and experience and on the size and nature of the Area.

c. *Regions* will have overall responsibility for supplies policies and procedures Many Areas will be relatively small (nearly 40 percent of the Areas outside London may not be divided into Districts) and it may well be advantageous for Areas to work together for supply purposes. Better prices and economies in storage costs and stock levels may be possible if Areas combine to place orders and arrange storage and distribution facilities. A Regional Supplies Officer will be accountable to the Administrator for the Regional supplies function, which includes:
—Determining the appropriate organisational level at which to negotiate terms, place orders, store and distribute goods.
—Promoting the rationalisation of supplies and equipment and, for certain items* (to be agreed with AHAs) preparing specifications and negotiating terms. In very special cases i.e. highly specialised equipment or drugs, the Region might itself store and distribute stocks to users.
—Establishing quality control procedures and issuing advice and guidance to Area staff.

The Supplies Officer will need some supporting staff. As with the Area supplies organisation, allocation of responsibilities between officers can only be determined by each RHA in the light of the calibre and experience of its staff and the particular problems facing it.

B. PROVIDING ADMINISTRATIVE SERVICES

11.11.   AAs and RAs will provide secretarial support to their Authorities and, in the case of the AA, to the FPC. In addition, administrative staff have important roles to play in supporting their colleagues and members of other professions with advice on personnel management, management services, public relations and legal problems. Administrators also provide office accommodation and services for health services staff. The organisation to carry out each of these functions is described in detail below:

* Regional supplies staff will be particularly concerned with equipment for capital projects.

(1) Providing services for Family Practitioner Committees

11.12.   The routine responsibilities of FPCs are largely the same as those of the present Executive Councils. The internal administrative organisation of FPCs will be similar therefore to the present arrangements. The FPC will not be a separate employing Authority and the Secretary of the Committee* will be a member of the AA's staff attached to the Committee, to which he will be operationally accountable. The Committee will, however, be consulted on all senior appointments to its staff. Finance staff will be attached to the Committee's administrator and will be under his operational control. It will be from him that they receive authority for the payments to be made to the practitioners under contract, and to him that they will be accountable for the prompt making of those payments.

(2) Personnel services

11.13.   The personnel function embraces recruitment, advising on the determination of organisation structure and development and management of staff. It includes all aspects of manpower information and planning, assessment of staffing requirements and staff complements, promotion and appointments arrangements, training and career development, with associated staff appraisal and counselling, negotiation of pay and other conditions of service and arrangements for consultation with staff interests and for the welfare of staff. It also includes the activities arising in the working situation, such as consultation and grievance and disciplinary procedures. Some of these activities e.g. negotiation of pay and conditions of service, will be carried out nationally. However, most of the responsibility will rest with professional staff and line managers working in the field who will, however, clearly require expert specialist advice on aspects of the personnel function.

11.14.   This advice and support will come from professional colleagues and from a strengthened personnel services function:

a.   *At District level*, an administrator on the staff of the General Administrator will carry out local personnel work, largely connected with the mechanics of employment of staff. In addition, in large Districts full-time personnel experts will be required. These will be attached to the District from the Area personnel department (see below) and will be operationally accountable to the DA.

b.   *At Area level*, an Area Personnel Officer, accountable to the AA, will have the following main responsibilities in support of the Area Team of Officers and DMTs:
—To assist District managers to assess the effect on numbers and levels of staff of proposed changes in the nature and scale of local health services.
—To help with the local recruitment effort and provide administrative support necessary to facilitate the recruitment of staff at Area and District levels.
—To advise managers on personnel policy questions generally e.g. on the implementation of nationally agreed pay and grading structures, the

* Described as the Administrator (Family Practitioner Services).

installation of productivity schemes, changes in staff organisation, the local implications of new legislation affecting employment and on staff welfare and industrial relations.

—To support managers in developing the skills and management ability of their staff i.e. by training and career development.

c. *At Regional, level* a Regional Personnel Officer, accountable to the RA, will have the following main functions in support of the Regional Team of Officers:

—As part of the planning process, to assist the Regional Medical Officer and Regional Nursing Officer forecast Regional manpower requirements for selected groups of staff, for submission to the RHA and subsequent discussion with the DHSS. He will help to allocate to AHAs increases agreed by DHSS.

—To review and evaluate AHA proposals for increases in total establishments, changes to the agreed scheme of management or variations from agreed pay and conditions of service and to recommend RHA action.

—To build on the counselling and career development work of the National Staff Committee and extend this to other groups of staff where this will be appropriate e.g. works professionals, ambulance staff, etc.

—To promote management and supervisory training for all the senior staff within the Region, co-ordinate Area training activities and provide, with the assistance of training specialists, expert advice on training questions, running Regional training where this is required.

—To provide machinery for hearing appeals on disciplinary procedures and for dealing with industrial relations questions arising at Regional level.

(3) Providing management services

11.15. There are three main kinds of specialist management services required by professional staff and line managers; organisation and method and work study activities, management consultancy, and statistics and computer services. Usually management services staff will be providing advice to line managers and to be effective in this they will need to have, for all aspects of their work, clearly recognised customers, able and willing to use the information provided.

11.16. Some important constraints have been taken into account in formulating proposals for the organisation of management services in a reorganised Health Service. People with the required skills and experience are in short supply and it will often be desirable to provide specialist management services in collaboration with local authorities. Moreover, there are disadvantages in organising services in small outposted units; in particular, staff have less contact with their professional colleagues and supervision is more difficult, and the variety of work is often insufficient to maintain their interest and develop their skills. Management services will, therefore, normally be confined to Area and Regional levels.

a. *At District level* there will not normally be a management services capability. Districts will look to the Area or Region for management services'

109

advice and support; and management services staff will be attached or outposted to the DA if required. The exception is likely to be teaching and other large Districts. In such cases, a Management Services Officer might be appointed, accountable to the DA.

b. *At Area level*, provision of management services will vary according to the size and needs of the Area. In most Areas, management services staff, headed by a Management Services Officer, who would either be subordinate to the AA or seconded to him by the Region, will be available. In larger Areas, experts in operational research, statistics or computers, might also be made available, depending on local needs and taking into account the constraints on local deployment of management services staff.

c. *Regions* will continue to provide most of the management services support to Areas in management consultancy, statistics, operational research and computers. They will also provide work study and O and M staff for smaller Areas which do not justify permanent provision of these skills. Regional management services staff will also help to develop norms and standards of performance and to produce inter-Area comparisons on the use of manpower and material resources. The Regional management services organisation will be headed by a Management Services Officer accountable to the RA.

(4) Legal and public relations services

11.17.   Health Authorities will require legal advice on a wide range of problems, by no means all of them specifically health problems. For example, the work of legal advisers to present RHBs includes responsibility for advising the Authority on questions related to master and servant and employers' liability, conveyancing and the legal aspects of estate management, contract, road traffic matters, trusts, charities and some aspects of the administration of deceased persons' estates. There is no need to provide specialist advisers at Area level. AAs will be responsible for identifying the need for legal services and for seeing that these are readily available when required. But the service itself, however, should come from a legal adviser, co-ordinated by the RA, or from outside advisers retained on the advice of the Region.

11.18.   Similarly, specialist public relations support e.g. photographers, etc. to Area and District staff will be provided by a Public Relations Officer accountable to the RA. This does not mean, however, that the Region needs to be consulted every time members of the press or public seek information about local services. Quite the contrary. One of the benefits of the integration of health services should be a wider awareness among the public of work going on in the District and contacts between health services staff, the local press and special interest groups will continue and expand. Where necessary, DAs and AAs will co-ordinate local public relations activities.

Finally, the Administrators at District, Area and Region will provide secretarial support to the DMT, AHA and RHA, and accommodation and office services. At District and Area, these will be the responsibility of an administrative assistant, accountable to the General Administrator. At the RHA they will form part of the responsibilities of the RHA secretariat.

C. PROVIDING GENERAL ADMINISTRATIVE CO-ORDINATION

11.19. The third major function of administrators in the Health Service is that of general co-ordination i.e. helping all branches of the Service to work effectively together to meet patient needs. This is particularly important where so many independent professions are involved, and in an organisation built around multi-disciplinary teams which, by definition are "consensus" groups with no power to impose their joint views on individual team members. Co-ordination of this sort will be required at all levels in the Service:

a. *At unit or sector level*, the various institutional and support services must be co-ordinated with the clinical support* and diagnostic† services, and with primary care and hospital services provided by professional staff treating patients. Someone must also see that the plans for different support services are mutually consistent and that they are co-ordinated on a day-to-day basis.

b. *At District level*, the work of the DMT must be co-ordinated. This will involve:
   —Seeing that plans for District institutional, support and administrative services are developed and co-ordinated with each other and successfully implemented.
   —Ensuring that team members have the administrative staff assistance necessary to enable them to draw up their individual aspects of a District plan and to meet their administrative responsibilities.
   —Co-ordinating the total planning process. This entails that the various aspects of the planning process, for which team members and their sub-ordinates have individual co-ordinating responsibility, are co-ordinated with each other within an overall programme.
   —Putting together the team's agreed proposals and options for discussion with the Area staff and subsequently for presentation to the AHA.

c. *At Area level*, there is also a need for general co-ordination. Area institutional, support and administrative services must be co-ordinated with each other and the Area staff must ensure that services are co-ordinated between Districts.
   —The Area planning process must be co-ordinated, and AHA plans must take into account the intentions of the matching local authority providing social services.
   —Area officers must provide co-ordinated advice and support to the AHA and its FPC and ensure that FPC and AHA plans are consistent with each other.

d. *Similarly, at Regional level*, Regional administrative services must be co-ordinated with each other and with AHA services, and officers must work together as a team to develop agreed service plans and capital development programmes for submission to the RHA, to monitor AHA performance effectively and evaluate AHA plans.

* E.g. medical records, outpatients, admissions, accident and emergency services, operating theatres.
† E.g. pathology, radiology, radiotherapy, EEG, clinical chemistry and photography.

11.20.   Responsibility for securing this general co-ordination will rest with the senior administrator at each level of organisation.

11.21.   Throughout this Chapter, no reference has been made to the administrative arrangements in an Area not divided into Districts i.e. a one-District Area. These will be exactly the same as in Exhibit XII, except that the DA becomes the AA and will be supported by the Administrator (Family Practitioner Services), a Personnel Officer, Management Services Officer and a Chief Ambulance Officer (if the ambulance service is being provided by the AHA).

APPENDIX 1

DEFINING DISTRICTS AND DEALING WITH PROBLEMS OF OVERLAP

1.   It will be necessary to define the boundaries of the "health" District— one of the key features of organisation introduced in Chapter 1. This presents problems, since inevitably there will be places that are physically in one Area but look for their hospital services to another. For example, although Henley-on-Thames will be in the Oxfordshire Area, over 90 percent of Henley residents requiring inpatient treatment receive it in Reading, which is in the Berkshire Area. This "overlap" problem will arise in many places. This Appendix suggests methods for determining District boundaries and dealing with any "overlap" problems that arise.

A. DEFINING DISTRICT BOUNDARIES

2.   The determination of Districts will be influenced by geography e.g. whether urban or rural, by the state of development of services e.g. the DGH, health centres, group practices and attachment schemes, and by whether there is continued use of large psychiatric hospitals and other longstay institutions. Although District boundaries will not inhibit the right of individual practitioners to refer their patients to the hospital and consultant of their choice, nevertheless one of the major objects of integration is to progress towards a closer and more effective partnership between primary and secondary care. Therefore, Districts must take account of the way in which it is planned to develop comprehensive health services in the future, as well as existing patterns of services such as the flows of patients from general practitioners to particular hospitals, and these plans will themselves take account of natural affinities.

3.   In general, the guiding principle will be that the District should contain the smallest population for which a realistic plan can be developed for the provision of integrated services to satisfy most health care needs. Ideally, each District should meet the following four requirements:

a. *Population of 200,000–300,000.* This size of population is generally held to be large enough to permit economical provision of a district general hospital and the normal range of specialities. It is about the right size for interaction between general medical and dental practitioners and their specialist colleagues, and for effective use of representative systems for clinicians i.e. consultants and general practitioners. These become unwieldy unless numbers are limited.

b. *Be largely self-contained and detached.* Ideally, people should be able to look to district general hospitals within the District for hospital care. Each District should, therefore, contain the normal range of major specialities, be largely self-sufficient in terms of professional staff and have its own postgraduate medical centre as the meeting place of the health-care professions.

c. *Correspond both with local authority district boundaries and with operational divisions of social work departments.* This will facilitate the necessary co-operation on the ground between health services, particularly district nurses, health visitors and domiciliary midwives, the social services provided by the counties or metropolitan districts and the health education and environmental health services of district authorities.

d. *Take existing patient flow patterns into account.* It may be tempting to establish District boundaries arbitrarily in the hope that general medical practitioners will adjust their referral arrangements and that hospital services will develop so that "natural" districts evolve. So they may; but arrangements for 1974 must recognise present realities as well as future aspirations.

4.   In establishing District boundaries, therefore, AHAs should first examine data on existing patient flows, using HIPE and HAA information, modifying the existing pattern in the light of future plans. This will identify those sections of the population which are consistently referred to particular DGHs. The second stage should then be to modify the district pattern identified by the first analysis to take account of other arrangements. These include the present management structures e.g. "Cogwheel" and "Salmon" and administrative groupings, future plans for hospital building, pattern of local authority services (and particularly, in urban areas, the boundaries for social services "area" teams), local transport patterns, and population trends and other demographic considerations.

5.   This analysis should normally result in Districts which are already served by a single DGH or teaching hospital or their equivalent, or which will be served by a new DGH. However, there will be exceptions to this "normal" District. An examination of seven Areas has shown that some Districts may be as small as 100,000 population, whereas others might be over 400,000. Moreover, though District boundaries will, so far as possible, fall within the Area boundaries, nevertheless, the natural pattern of comprehensive health care will often overlap the Area boundary and special arrangements may be necessary.

B. DEALING WITH OVERLAP PROBLEMS

6.   Districts, as defined above, may tend to overlap AHA boundaries, in some cases marginally but in others significantly. Essentially there are two kinds of overlap:

113

(1) *Inconvenient Area boundaries*, i.e. situations in which the Area boundaries do not match the "natural" District boundaries, so that part of a District's catchment population and its health resources are situated within the Area of a different AHA.

(2) *Specialist hospital catchment Areas not matching District at all*. For example, a single mental handicap hospital may serve a large number of Districts, or the mental illness hospital on which a District will rely may be situated right away from it, even in a different Region. This problem has nothing to do with the way Area boundaries are drawn. It could arise between the several Districts within a single Area. The fact that there may also be an Area or Regional boundary separating a District from, for example, its mental illness hospital is only an additional complication.

The two kinds of situation give rise to a similar problem, but they have different causes and may be solved differently, as described below. Whatever arrangements are made, general practitioners, who habitually send their patients to a DGH which will be across the Area boundary, must be able to continue to do so and must be able to maintain and develop necessary working links with their DGH.

(1) Inconvenient Area boundaries.

7. Within this first category, there are several gradations of the problem. An overlap zone may occur where much of the population uses the DGH situated within another AHA, and where there are also GPs who generally send most of their patients across the Area boundary line. In addition, the overlap zone may contain some "managed" NHS resources, e.g. community nurses, or peripheral or community hospitals, or even parts of the DGH complex itself.

8. Overlap zones containing patients and GPs, but not managed resources, present some organisational questions. For example, to which AHA and FPC should such GPs be attached, and on which District Medical Committee and DMT should they be represented? There are three possible arrangements:
   a. Such GPs remain attached to the FPC of the Area from which they would ordinarily draw their payment and are represented on the DMC and DMT of the nearest District of this AHA.
   b. They remain so attached but are primarily, or exclusively, represented on the DMC and DMT of their "natural" District.
   c. They are attached to the FPC of the Area to which their "natural" District belongs and are represented on its DMC and DMT only.

It will be for the responsible AHA concerned, in consultation with local clinicians, to decide which arrangement is in the best interests of their patients.

9. A more difficult problem is presented by zones that include not only GPs but also some "managed" health resources, such as community nurses and small hospitals. Such zones can be quite large and will usually lie unequivocally within one Area or another, and here it seriously matters what administrative arrangements are made. There appear to be three possible management patterns that could be applied, individually or in combination, to such resources:
   a. Clinicians and staff working in the overlap zone can be employed by, or be in contract with the FPC of, the AHA of the Area in which they are

working. This AHA would finance the services, which would be managed by the DMT of its nearest District. The necessary co-ordination with the "natural" district would be achieved by informal consultative arrangements.

b. Clinicians and staff working in the overlap zone can be employed by or in contract with, and thus financed by this same AHA (or its FPC), to which the zone physically belongs, but participate in the management of the "natural" District. This could be achieved by permanently seconding staff from the AHA "of origin" to the AHA providing most of the services to people living in the overlap zone.

c. By contrast clinicians and staff working in the overlap zone can be employed by, or be in contract with, the AHA, or FPC, of the "natural" District. The AHA of this District would finance the services, which would be managed as a wholly integrated part of the "natural" District by the DMT. The AHA whose population live in the overlap zone, would be providing health services for them through the agency of another AHA. The RHA would then allocate resources between the two AHAs accordingly. Similarly, DHSS will take any overlap arrangements into account if two RHAs are involved. Thus, no inter-AHA, or inter-RHA, recharges will be necessary.

10.   In the last case, the AHA, or RHA, that receives services from its neighbouring Authority is still fulfilling its duty, in that it is "securing the provision" of health care to its population, even though not providing it directly. The AHA receiving the services, as well as that providing the service, can also maintain a monitoring role over the overall quality of health care provided to overlap zones.

(2) Specialty hospitals not corresponding to Districts

11.   There will be many cases where special, generally long-stay, hospitals serve a catchment population that covers several Districts, or where the hospital that mainly, if not exclusively, serves one District lies right outside that District. This has nothing to do with the way Area boundaries are drawn and could occur entirely within one Area, only affecting the division of responsibilities between the Districts within that Area. The goal is that both mental-illness and mental-handicap services should eventually be planned on a District basis. In the meantime the difficulty will persist in many places. For example, although there will probably be two health Districts in North Nottinghamshire, neither will have long-stay accommodation for the mentally ill, and much of the accommodation for the mentally handicapped for the whole Area will be provided from outside Nottinghamshire.

12.   More than one DMT will have a direct interest in the care provided by such hospitals, but the hospitals can only be managed by one management. There seems to be no alternative but to assign management responsibility for such hospitals to the most convenient DMT, i.e. that of the District within which the hospitals lie, with the RHA and AHA allocating resources to that District accordingly. As a result, some DMTs will manage no psychiatric hospitals, but this does not prevent the Districts from having mental-health planning teams in the District, or the AHAs concerned from working with their matching local authorities to plan services.

115

APPENDIX 2

ORGANISATION AND OPERATION OF THE DEPARTMENT OF HEALTH AND SOCIAL SECURITY

1. The organisation and operation of the health and personal social services parts of the Department of Health and Social Security has been reviewed. Proposals have been formulated which are designed to enable the Department to carry out effectively the functions it will have after NHS reorganisation. The recommendations are based closely on the Department's role, which is to support the Secretary of State in the following ways:
   a. In his government, parliamentary and public duties.
   b. In the determination of national objectives, priorities and standards, and allocation of resources, so far as this should and can be done at national level, for the health and social services.
   c. In guiding, supporting and (to the extent that this is within his powers and desirable) controlling (i) the Health Authorities and (ii) the local authorities, in their running of the health and social services.
   d. In obtaining or developing resources that strongly influence the adequacy, efficiency and economy of the services.

2. The organisation recommended for the Department has two principal features:
   a. Six main organisational groups of administrative and professional staff are defined in terms of the work that must be done to meet the principal requirements of the Department's responsibilities and operation (which are stated above).
   b. Separate organisational hierarchies are preserved for the different disciplines (professional and administrative), but each hierarchy is related closely to a common work structure so that the disciplines can most easily work in partnership.

The six organisational groups and their main purposes are shown in Exhibit XV.

3. As part of its method of operation, it is proposed to introduce a planning system which will help the Department, in association with Health Authorities and local authorities, to assist the Secretary of State decide national objectives and priorities. One of the six organisational commands, the *Services Development Group*, will be primarily responsible for developing national policy to improve health and personal social services and will play a major part in the planning process. It will give special attention to assessing people's overall needs. In the Group will be branches concerned with particular groups of people such as the elderly, the physically handicapped, the mentally disordered and children, but it is proposed that the emphasis in all branches should be on people's needs for services and how these can best be met.

4. Another organisational command, The *Regional Group*, will be the main link with RHAs and local authorities and will be organised on a geographical basis. This Group will assist Health Authorities to produce and implement plans which will give effect to national policies while taking full account of local circumstances, priorities and policies. It will also ensure that Health Authorities receive any help that they need from the Department. More staff than in the past

116

Exhibit XV

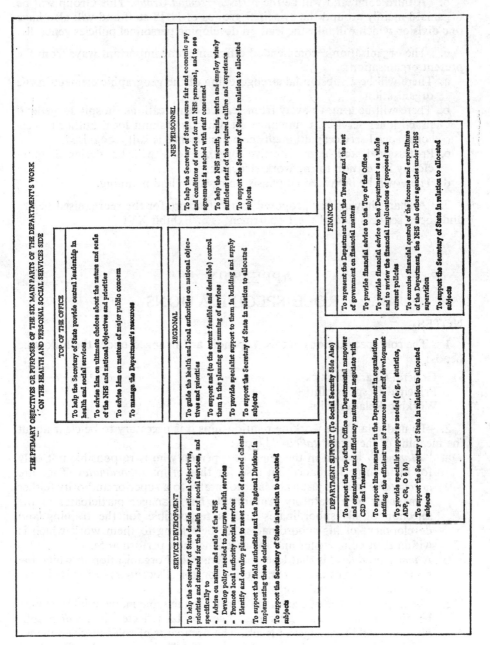

THE PRIMARY OBJECTIVES OR PURPOSES OF THE SIX MAIN PARTS OF THE DEPARTMENT'S WORK
ON THE HEALTH AND PERSONAL SOCIAL SERVICES SIDE

TOP OF THE OFFICE

To help the Secretary of State provide central leadership in health and social services

To advise him on ultimate choices about the nature and scale of the NHS and national objectives and priorities

To advise him on matters of major public concern

To manage the Department's resources

NHS PERSONNEL

To help the Secretary of State secure fair and economic pay and conditions of service for all NHS personnel, and to see agreement is reached with staff concerned

To help the NHS recruit, train, retrain and employ wisely sufficient staff of the required calibre and experience

To support the Secretary of State in relation to allocated subjects

REGIONAL

To guide the health and local authorities on national objectives and priorities

To support and (to the extent feasible and desirable) control them in the planning and running of services

To provide specialist support to them in building and supply

To support the Secretary of State in relation to allocated subjects

FINANCE

To represent the Department with the Treasury and the rest of government on financial matters

To provide financial advice to the Top of the Office

To provide financial advice to the Department as a whole and to review the financial implications of proposed and current policies

To exercise financial control of the income and expenditure of the Department, the NHS and other agencies under DHSS supervision

To support the Secretary of State in relation to allocated subjects

SERVICE DEVELOPMENT

To help the Secretary of State decide national objectives, priorities and standards for the health and social services, and specifically to

-   Advise on nature and scale of the NHS
-   Develop policy needed to improve health services
-   Promote local authority social services
-   Identify and develop plans to meet needs of selected clients

To support the field authorities and the Regional Divisions in implementing these decisions

To support the Secretary of State in relation to allocated subjects

DEPARTMENT SUPPORT (To Social Security Side Also)

To support the Top of the Office on Departmental manpower and organisation and efficiency matters and negotiate with CSD and Treasury

To support line managers in the Department in organisation, staffing, the efficient use of resources and staff development

To provide specialist support as needed (e.g., statistics, ADP, OR, O & M)

To support the Secretary of State in relation to allocated subjects will be allocated to this work. They will normally be centrally-based, not out-posted.

5. A third command will be the *NHS Personnel Group*. This Group will be organised mainly around the principal groups of NHS staff and will also have one division which will take the lead on developing personnel policies generally.

6. The organisation recommended differs in some important ways from the present organisation:

  a. There will be a substantial strengthening of the geographic element in the organisation.
  b. There will be a move away from service demarcations (hospitals, general practitioner services, community health services and local authority personal social services) although their importance is still recognised.
  c. Professional and administrative organisations will be designed more closely in relation to the work structure.
  d. There will be increased emphasis on research and planning.

7. A chart showing the proposed work structure for the reorganised health and social services side of the Department is at Exhibit XVI.

APPENDIX 3

ROLE SPECIFICATIONS

NOTES

1. The role specifications in this Appendix are arranged under the following heads:

  General Characteristics
  Principal Responsibilities
  Working Relationships

2. To understand the working relationships it is necessary to be clear about the meaning of the terms *italicised* below:

  a. "*Manager*" is used in the sense of a person who is responsible not only for his own performance but also for that of his *subordinates*. They are *accountable* to him, just as he is accountable to a superior authority (either a manager or a statutory Authority). The manager participates in the selection of his subordinates and is responsible for the training and development of his subordinates, for delegating to them work which is within their competence and for assessing their performance.
  b. A *managerial level* is that level in a hierarchical organisation in which the occupants of roles are in managerial control of occupants of roles in the next lower managerial level.
  c. The responsibilities of occupants of roles in the same managerial level may be different and these differences need to be reflected in *grading* subdivisions within managerial levels. The occupants of roles in given managerial levels may manage the occupants of roles in any grade of the level below, but cannot manage occupants of roles in a lower grade of the same level.

EXHIBIT XVI

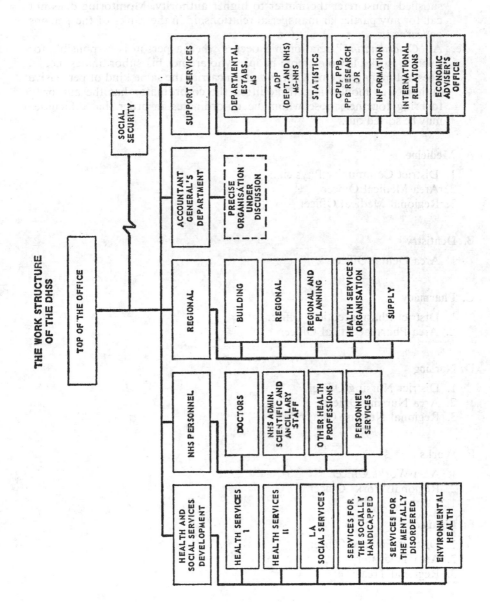

THE WORK STRUCTURE
OF THE DHSS

d. A "*Monitoring*" relationship is not managerial. The person who monitors has the authority to require to be kept informed about the activities of the persons monitored and has authority to persuade them to change but, in the final analysis, he cannot order them to do anything and, if not satisfied, must refer the matter to higher authority. Monitoring does not call for any particular managerial relationship in the ranks of the persons concerned.

e. A "*Co-ordinating*" relationship occurs when a person is responsible for relating work of two or more people who are not his subordinates (i.e. he does not manage them). Co-ordination carries the same kind of persuasive authority as monitoring. In addition the co-ordinator has the authority to bring together those whom he co-ordinates in order that difficulties may be sorted out.

A. Medicine

1. District Community Physician
2. Area Medical Officer
3. Regional Medical Officer

B. Dentistry

1. Area Dental Officer

C. Pharmacy

1. District Pharmaceutical Officer
2. Area Pharmaceutical Officer

D. Nursing

1. District Nursing Officer
2. Area Nursing Officer
3. Regional Nursing Officer

E. Works

1. Area Works Officer
2. Regional Works Officer

F. Finance

1. District Finance Officer
2. Area Treasurer
3. Regional Treasurer

G. Administration and allied skills

1. District Administrator
2. District Support Services Manager
3. Sector Administrator

4. Area Administrator
5. Administrator (Family Practitioner Committee)
6. Area Personnel Officer
7. Area Supplies Officer
8. Regional Administrator
9. Regional Supplies Officer
10. Regional Personnel Officer
11. Administrator (Capital Building Programme)
12. Administrator (Regional Service Planning)
13. Regional Ambulance Officer

DISTRICT COMMUNITY PHYSICIAN

GENERAL CHARACTERISTICS

The District Community Physician will be a member of the DMT and will be engaged in four main spheres of activity: (a) co-ordinating the formulation of plans for the operational health care services; (b) advising his clinical colleagues as a specialist in community medicine; (c) co-ordinating the preventive services; and (d) carrying out various functions for local authorities.

PRINCIPAL RESPONSIBILITIES

1. Co-ordinates service planning

1.1 Continuously assesses the community's need for health care and maintains a health profile of the District.

1.2 Keeps under review the provision of services within the District and identifies gaps in relation to need.

1.3 Identifies opportunities to improve medical services, so as to provide the best patient care with the resources available.

1.4 Co-ordinates the various health-care planning teams, so as to ensure that sound proposals for change are prepared for the DMT within the guidelines established by it.

1.5 Organises or conducts special studies for the DMT in relation to the operational health-care services.

1.6 Maintains a general surveillance of the implementation of improvement projects, with particular reference to the assessment of the effectiveness of changes in service organisation or methods.

1.7 Works closely with the District Medical Committee and its divisions in drawing up plans for medical services.

2. Advises his colleagues as a specialist

Stimulates the process of integration, by advising his consultant and general practitioner colleagues in his capacity as a specialist in community medicine. Makes available his knowledge of the needs of the District and his expertise in the organisation of health-care and epidemiological techniques.

3. Co-ordinates various preventive services

3.1 Controls the work of clinical medical officers attached to him by the Area Medical Officer to provide preventive services, including vaccination and immunisation, and screening.

3.2 Plans and co-ordinates the work of medical officers in school health services where this responsibility is assigned to him by the Area Medical Officer.

3.3 Arranges for the provision of some preventive services by general practitioners, either in their own premises or in AHA clinics.

3.4 Arranges, when appropriate, for consultant sessions in preventive clinics throughout the District.

3.5 Ensures that the health education programmes, managed by the Area Medical Officer, are co-ordinated with the general preventive services of the District.

4. **Functions in relation to the local authority**

4.1 In certain Districts he is likely to be invited to act as the proper officer on environmental health matters to a local government district authority.*

4.2 Carries out certain functions assigned to him by the Area Medical Officer in relation to the local authority's retained responsibilities for school health.

WORKING RELATIONSHIPS

Accountable to: Area Health Authority†

Manages: Attached clinical medical officers

                                      Attached administrative staff

Monitored and co-ordinated by: Area Medical Officer

---

* He will be accountable directly to a local authority when he is acting as their proper officer on environmental health.

† He will be responsible to the Area Medical Officer for carrying out any school health functions assigned to him.

AREA MEDICAL OFFICER

GENERAL CHARACTERISTICS

The Area Medical Officer will be a member of the Area Team of Officers and will advise the AHA, both as a member of the team and as an independent source of medical advice. He will be engaged in five main spheres of activity: (a) co-ordinating the formulation of advice to the AHA on policies and plans for the operational health-care services; (b) co-ordinating the formulation of joint service plans with the matching local authority; (c) co-ordinating preventive-care services throughout the Area; (d) monitoring and co-ordinating District performance; and (e) carrying out various functions for the matching local authorities.

PRINCIPAL RESPONSIBILITIES

1. **Co-ordinates policy formulation and planning (as a member of the Area Team of Officers)**

   1.1 Keeps under review the health-care needs of the population of the Area as a whole and initiates special studies and research.

   1.2 Recommends appropriate Area operational health-care policies, after review of both national and Regional policy initiatives, policy proposals submitted by DMTs and by matching local authority.

   1.3 Draws up planning guidelines on Area operational health-care policies and priorities for DMTs.

   1.4 Reviews and challenges District plans and budgets for the operational health-care services.

   1.5 Provides specialist planning assistance and support to the District Community Physician, the District health-care planning teams and the DMT.

   1.6 Ensures the provision of adequate advice on medical aspects of plans for capital projects.

   1.7 Advises the AHA on how to use its medical advisory machinery effectively (convening specialist advisory groups as required, in consultation with the Medical Advisory Committee).

2. **Joint planning functions with local authority**

   The Area Medical Officer will be a member of the officer team of the joint consultative committees. He will:

   2.1 Co-ordinate the formulation of joint plans for the operational health-care services, in conjunction with the Area Nursing Officer and chief officers of the local authority.

   2.2 Carry out special analysis and research for the joint consultative committees.

   2.3 See that the policies and plans for the operational health-care services agreed by the joint consultative committees are properly taken account of by DMTs.

3. **Co-ordinates preventive and other services**

    3.1 Plans and manages the work of subordinate medical officers based at Area engaged in clinical work for infants and pre-school children, the school health services and other forms for screening.

    3.2 Co-ordinates all aspects of health services for children including speech therapy throughout the Area.

    3.3 Plans and provides health education and chiropody programmes for the population of the Area.

    3.4 Co-ordinates the dental and pharmaceutical services within the overall health services of the Area.

    3.5 Co-ordinates the planning of scientific services.

4. **Monitors and co-ordinates District performance**

    4.1 Reviews information, reports on and monitors and co-ordinates the performance of DMTs, particularly in relation to the operational health-care services and the function of the District Community Physician.

    4.2 Assists in the design and implementation of improved information for monitoring.

5. **Functions in relation to local authority**

    5.1 Likely to be invited to act as proper officer for environmental health to the relevant local authorities.*

    5.2 Likely to be invited to act as medical adviser to the local authority in relation to personal social services and school health.

6. **Provides personnel services**

In an AHA(T), provides the necessary personnel functions for consultants and senior registrars.

WORKING RELATIONSHIPS

Accountable to:	Area Health Authority†
Manages:	Area specialists in community medicine
	Clinical medical officers
	Attached administrative staff
	Health Education Officer
	Area Chiropodist
	Area Speech Therapist
Monitors and co-ordinates:	District Community Physician(s)
	Area Dental Officer
	Area Pharmaceutical Officer
Monitors:	Area Ambulance Officer (medical aspects only)
Monitored and co-ordinated by:	Regional Medical Officer
Member of Area Team of Officers	

   * In certain areas only.
   † He will also be accountable to the local authority for the performance of functions relating to them.

REGIONAL MEDICAL OFFICER

GENERAL CHARACTERISTICS

The Regional Medical Officer will be a member of the Regional Team of Officers and will advise the RHA, both as a member of the team and as an independent source of medical advice. He will be engaged in five main spheres of activity: (a) co-ordinating the formulation of advice to the RHA on policies and plans for the operational health-care services; (b) co-ordinating the briefing stage of major capital building projects; (c) monitoring and co-ordinating Area performance; (d) co-ordinating research, postgraduate education, etc.; and (e) providing personnel services for consultants and senior registrars.

1. **Co-ordinates policy formulation and planning (as a member of the Regional Team of Officers)**

   1.1 Maintains an inventory of the health-care needs of the Region as a whole, based both on locally-identified needs and on special Regional studies.

   1.2 Co-ordinates the formulation of Regional policies related to the development of the operational health-care services of the Region, including the distribution of medical specialities and the deployment of medical manpower, and scheduling of major capital building projects.

   1.3 Co-ordinates the work of any multi-disciplinary Regional health-care planning teams established to review services directed towards specific groups of needs.

   1.4 Draws up planning guidelines on Regional health-care policies and priorities for each AHA, and communicates these guidelines to Area Medical Officers.

   1.5 Reviews and challenges AHA plans and budgets for the operational health-care services in relation to the agreed guidelines.

   1.6 Provides specialist planning assistance for Area Medical Officers, including helping them to support District Community Physicians and District health-care planning teams.

   1.7 Advises the RHA on how to use its medical advisory machinery and ensures that the Regional Medical Advisory Committee is appropriately involved in the planning process.

   1.8 Reviews and modifies as necessary arrangements for overlap between AHAs, and the distribution of Regional and sub-Regional specialties.

   1.9 Reviews the extent to which collaboration is taking place between AHAs and their matching local authorities.

2. **Briefs project teams on capital projects**

   2.1 Provides medical advice to project teams concerned with capital building projects.

   2.2 Co-ordinates the briefing stage of major capital building projects.*

* I.e. those projects for which briefing is essentially dependent on the operational policies for medical services.

3. **Monitors and co-ordinates AHAs**

   3.1   Reviews information and reports on AHA performance.

   3.2   Monitors and co-ordinates the performance of Area Teams of Officers, particularly in relation to the operational health-care services and the functions of the Area Medical Officer.

   3.3   Assists in the design and implementation of Regional information and monitoring systems.

4. **Co-ordinates various Regional services**

   4.1   Co-ordinates the work of the Director of the Regional Blood Transfusion Service.

   4.2   Manages the work of the Regional Scientific Officer and the Regional Pharmaceutical Officer.

   4.3   Co-ordinates the development of postgraduate medical education, in conjunction with the postgraduate committee and postgraduate dean.

   4.4   Assists in determining priorities for the use of RHA funds available for health-care research, and co-ordinates community medicine research in liaison with the departments of social medicine and of general practice of the associated medical school.

5. **Provides personnel services**

Provides the necessary personnel services for Regionally employed consultants and senior registrars.

WORKING RELATIONSHIPS

Accountable to:	Regional Health Authority
Manages:	Regional specialists in community medicine
	Attached administrative staff
	Regional Scientific Officer
	Regional Pharmaceutical Officer
Monitors and co-ordinates:	Area Medical Officers
	Director Regional Blood Transfusion Service
Monitors:	Regional Ambulance Officer (medical aspects only)

Member of Regional Team of Officers

AREA DENTAL OFFICER

GENERAL CHARACTERISTICS

The Area Dental Officer is the dental adviser to the AHA and is responsible for planning and managing its salaried dental service and for monitoring and promoting the improvement of the overall standard of dental care within the Area.

PRINCIPAL RESPONSIBILITIES

1. **Advises the AHA on dental matters**
   Advises the AHA, the FPC (on matters not specifically the responsibility of the dental advisory body for the FPC) and the Area Team of Officers on all matters concerned with or having implications for dentistry.

2. **Advises the local authority**

   Advises the local authority on dental matters, particularly concerning the dental health of school children.

3. **Manages the AHA's salaried dental service**
   3.1 In collaboration with the local authority and the Area Medical Officer, recruits, deploys and organises the work of the AHA's salaried dental officers, to provide a comprehensive school dental service and a priority service for mothers and young children.
   3.2 Manages the auxiliary staff and other back-up resources necessary for this service, including the dental laboratory service.

4. **Promotes the improvement of the overall dental service**
   4.1 Monitors the dental service in the Area, including that provided by general dental practitioners and consultants, in relation to local needs and the standards and priorities laid down or agreed by the AHA.
   4.2 Proposes to the AHA plans to improve the service.
   4.3 Seeks the agreement of general dental practitioners and consultants to actions on their part that would improve the service.
   4.4 Co-ordinates the work of the Area's dental clinicians e.g. to ensure the provision of an adequate emergency dental service.

WORKING RELATIONSHIPS

Accountable to: Area Health Authority
Manages: Dental officers in employment of AHA
                                          Deputy Area Dental Officer, where applicable

	District Dental Officers, where applicable (in respect of their administrative work), and auxiliary dental staff employed by AHA
Relationship with Area Team of Officers:	Receives all team agendas, papers and minutes, and has a right to attend team meetings when matters which he considers critical to dentistry are to be discussed. He collaborates with the Area Medical Officer and the local authority concerned on the planning and execution of the dental part of the overall school health service.

DISTRICT PHARMACEUTICAL OFFICER

GENERAL CHARACTERISTICS

The District Pharmaceutical Officer manages pharmaceutical services in a District. He assists in their co-ordination with general practice pharmacy and advises the District Medical Committee and the DMT on pharmaceutical matters.

PRINCIPAL RESPONSIBILITIES

1. **Manages pharmaceutical services**
   1.1 Manages directly and through Principal and Staff Pharmacists the pharmaceutical services at hospitals and clinics.
   1.2 Maintains dispensing facilities at hospitals and clinics, including measures for security of drugs.

2. **Advises on pharmaceutical matters**
   2.1 Contributes to District plans for pharmaceutical services.
   2.2 Attends meetings of the DMT when matters affecting pharmacy are to be discussed.
   2.3 Advises medical staff, through the District Medical Committee, on pharmaceutical matters, including measures for economy in the use of medicines.
   2.4 Helps to co-ordinate the work of hospital and general practitioner pharmacists in the District.

WORKING RELATIONSHIPS

Accountable to:	Area Pharmaceutical Officer
Manages:	Principal and Staff Pharmacists
Co-ordinated by:	District Administrator on behalf of the DMT
Relationship with District Management Team:	Attends DMT meetings, as necessary.

AREA PHARMACEUTICAL OFFICER

GENERAL CHARACTERISTICS

The Area Pharmaceutical Officer is responsible for the management of pharmaceutical services, including quality control, for one or more Areas, and for their co-ordination with general practice pharmacy. He also assists in the provision of co-ordinated advice to the AHA and its officers.

PRINCIPAL RESPONSIBILITIES

1. **Provides and co-ordinates advice on pharmaceutical matters**

   1.1 Advises the AHA(s) to whom he is accountable for managing pharmaceutical services, any AHA to which he is giving a service, and the Area Team(s) of Officers, on policies concerning pharmacy.

   1.2 Contributes to Area and District plans for pharmacy.

   1.3 Attends meetings of the Area Team(s) of Officers and, unless there is a District Pharmaceutical Officer, the DMT(s) when matters affecting pharmacy are to be discussed.

   1.4 Acts as convenor of the Area Pharmaceutical Committee.

   1.5 Helps to co-ordinate advice to the AHA(s) and Area Team(s) of Officers on matters of interest to both general practitioners and hospital pharmacists.

   1.6 Advises District Medical Committees, either directly or through the District Pharmaceutical Officer or Pharmaceutical Officer, on pharmaceutical matters, including measures for economy in the use of medicines.

2. **Manages pharmaceutical services**

   2.1 Manages pharmaceutical services at hospitals and clinics:

   a. In an Area not divided into Districts, through outposted Principal and Staff Pharmacists;

   b. In an Area divided into Districts, through District Pharmaceutical Officers or, with the help of Pharmaceutical Officers, through outposted Principal and Staff Pharmacists;

   c. In any other Area for which he provides a service with the help of a Pharmaceutical Officer, through outposted Principal and Staff Pharmacists.

   2.2 Maintains dispensing facilities, including measures for security of medicines, in hospitals and clinics, calling on the services of chemists contractors in accordance with policy and Area plans.

131

WORKING RELATIONSHIPS

Accountable to: Area Health Authority

Manages: Principal and Staff Pharmacists (through District Pharmaceutical Officers, if appointed) and Pharmaceutical Officers (if any)

Monitored and Co-ordinated by: District Administrator and, in relation to medical activities, Area Medical Officer.

Relationship with Area Team of Officers: Attends meetings of the Area Team of Officers (and District Management Teams) as necessary; has right of access to the AHA and its Chairman.

DISTRICT NURSING OFFICER

GENERAL CHARACTERISTICS

The District Nursing Officer manages the nursing service in a District and is responsible for the maintenance of professional nursing standards. She has a functional co-ordinating responsibility and gives nursing advice to the DMT and to individual officers at District level. As a member of the DMT she participates in the planning of the health-care services of the District and plays a full role in the team's achievement of its objectives. She is directly accountable to the AHA.

PRINCIPAL RESPONSIBILITIES

1. Manages the nursing service in the District

1.1 Manages an integrated community and hospital nursing service, including the nursing budget.

1.2 Assesses needs and controls nursing performance and deployment against approved plans.

1.3 Initiates the formulation of nursing policies, and maintains a general surveillance of their implementation and the evaluation of their effectiveness. Ensures the co-ordination of nursing services with nurse education within the District.

1.4 Identifies opportunities to improve the quality of nursing services and care.

1.5 Ensures the appropriate use of personnel services by nursing managers, the effective operation of staff appraisal and training schemes and the provision of career development advice. Ensures that appropriate counselling advice is provided for nursing staff in the District.

1.6 Investigates the nursing aspects of accidents and complaints and participates in the development of corrective action. Establishes and reviews links with the Community Health Council and voluntary bodies.

1.7 As a member of the DMT, ensures the provision of support services for nursing in the District.

2. Gives nursing advice to the DMT

Advises on the process of integration and the implications of service proposals for nursing, and maintains professional standards and quality of care of patients.

3. Participates in planning of health-care services of the District

3.1 Participates, as a member of the DMT, in the formulation of the District plan and establishment of priorities. This includes identification of nursing needs in the light of service and educational requirements.

3.2 Ensures participation of nurses at all levels in multi-disciplinary team working, including membership of health-care planning teams.

133

WORKING RELATIONSHIPS

Accountable to: Area Health Authority

Manages: Community and hospital nursing staff in
the District

Attached non-nursing staff.

Monitored and co-ordinated by: Area Nursing Officer.

Member of District Management
    Team.

AREA NURSING OFFICER

GENERAL CHARACTERISTICS

The Area Nursing Officer is a member of the Area Team of Officers. She has a functional co-ordinating responsibility in relation to the team and plays a full role in the achievement of its objectives and the formulation of its plans and policies. She provides nursing advice to the AHA, to the Area Team of Officers, to individual officers at Area level and to the matching local authority. She monitors and co-ordinates the work of District Nursing Officers and manages nursing staff based at Area.

PRINCIPAL RESPONSIBILITIES

1. **Provides nursing advice to the AHA and its officers**
   1.1 Advises the AHA on professional nursing matters and, as a member of the Area Team of Officers, examines District plans for their implications for nursing and for their nursing content.
   1.2 Identifies the implications for the nursing services in the Area of DHSS and RHA policies and ensures that provision is made to accommodate the statutory requirements for nurse education.
   1.3 Co-ordinates the nursing function with other activities at Area level e.g. ensures appropriate support for the nursing service and participates, as a team member, in the development, use and review of supplies management information systems and management services.
   1.4 Develops priorities for the distribution of scarce and specialised nursing resources.
   1.5 Ensures that professional nursing and midwifery advisory machinery can work effectively.

2. **Participates in the planning of health-care services for the Area**
   2.1 Participates in the formulation of policies and plans, and the establishment of priorities for the Area and guidelines for DMTs.
   2.2 Participates in the review and challenge of District plans and budgets.
   2.3 Ensures the provision of adequate advice on the nursing aspects of plans for capital projects and Area works activities.

3. **Provides nursing advice to the matching local authority**
   3.1 Participates in the joint consultative process with the matching local authority.
   3.2 Monitors the provision by Districts of agreed services to local authorities and the professional aspects of services provided by staff seconded to the local authority.

4. **Monitors and co-ordinates the work of District Nursing Officers**

    4.1   Co-ordinates the work of District Nursing Officers and monitors their performance against Area guidelines and approved District plans.

    4.2   Supports and advises District Nursing Officers, as appropriate.

WORKING RELATIONSHIPS

Accountable to:	Area Health Authority
Manages:	Nursing Staff at Area Headquarters and outposted to Districts.
	Attached non-nursing staff.
Monitors and co-ordinates:	District Nursing Officers
Monitors and co-ordinated by:	Regional Nursing Officer.
Member of the Area Team of Officers.	

REGIONAL NURSING OFFICER

GENERAL CHARACTERISTICS

The Regional Nursing Officer is a member of the Regional Team of Officers and provides nursing advice to the RHA, to the Regional Team of Officers and to individual officers at Regional level. She has a functional co-ordinating responsibility and plays a full role in the team's achievements of its objectives. She monitors and co-ordinates the work of Area Nursing Officers and manages nursing staff based at Region.

PRINCIPAL RESPONSIBILITIES

1. **Provides nursing advice to the RHA and its officers**

    1.1 Advises the RHA on professional nursing matters and, as a member of the Regional Team of Officers, examines Area plans for their implications for nursing and their nursing content.

    1.2 Identifies the implications for the nursing services in the Region of DHSS policies and the requirements of statutory professional bodies.

    1.3 Advises the RHA on the nursing content of Regional services, including the development of priorities for the distribution of scarce and specialised nursing resources.

    1.4 Co-ordinates the nursing function with other activities at Regional level, e.g. participates in the development, use and review of supplies, management services and management information systems.

    1.5 Plans programmes of nursing research and development through liaison with Universities and other educational establishments.

    1.6 Ensures the appropriate use of agreed personnel services by nursing managers and provides counselling advice for nursing staff at Regional and Area level.

    1.7 Ensures that professional nursing and midwifery advisory machinery can work effectively.

2. **Participates in the planning of health-care services for the Region**

    2.1 Participates in the formulation of Regional policies and guidelines, and the establishment of priorities for AHAs.

    2.2 Participates in the review and challenge of AHA plans and budgets.

    2.3 Ensures nursing participation in multi-disciplinary service-planning teams to review specific needs. Ensures the provision of adequate briefing and adequate advice on the nursing aspects of plans for capital projects.

3. **Monitors and co-ordinates the work of Area Nursing Officers**

    3.1 Co-ordinates the work of Area Nursing Officers and monitors their performance against Regional guidelines and approved Area plans.

137

3.2 Ensures the effectiveness of collaboration on nursing matters between local authorities and AHAs.

3.3 Supports and advises Area Nursing Officers, as appropriate.

WORKING RELATIONSHIPS

Accountable to: Regional Health Authority

Manages: Region-based nursing staff and any staff out-posted to Areas.

Attached non-nursing staff.

Monitors and co-ordinates: Area Nursing Officers.

Member of Regional Team of Officers.

AREA WORKS OFFICER

GENERAL CHARACTERISTICS

The Area Works Officer provides a single point of contact on behalf of the works professions with the user or client professions within the Area. He provides advice to the Area Team of Officers and the AHA on works matters, is responsible for the building and engineering work delivered from Area and for the professional and technical standard of building and engineering throughout the Area, including within Districts. In smaller Areas these responsibilities will be carried out by an Engineer or a Building Officer at Area or District.

PRINCIPAL RESPONSIBILITIES

1. **Progresses the design and construction of capital works delegated from the RHA**

   1.1 Co-ordinates Area capital project teams during the stages of design and construction.

   1.2 Undertakes design of capital works, using design expertise from Region, outside consultants or local authority when necessary.

2. **Participates in the formulation of Area plans and budgets**

   2.1 Formulates plans for Area works activities, including building plans, programmes and budgets, and specialised maintenance to be delivered from Area.

   2.2 Seeks to ensure that District plans contain satisfactory programmes and budgets for maintenance.

   2.3 Ensures that Area plans take account of implications for building and engineering.

3. **Maintains standards of building and engineering work**

   Ensures that the building and engineering work carried out at District is of a satisfactory professional and technical standard.

WORKING RELATIONSHIPS

Accountable to:	Area Health Authority
Manages:	Area Building Officer
	Area Engineer
Monitored and Co-ordinated by:	Regional Works Officer
Monitors and Co-ordinates:	District Building Officer and District Engineer (in respect of the professional and technical content of their work).

Relationship with Area Team of Officers:

Receives all Area Team agendas, papers and minutes, and has the right to attend team meetings when matters which he considers critical to the works function are to be discussed. The Area Administrator will be responsible for ensuring that the work of Area Works Officer is co-ordinated with the work of the Area Team of Officers.

REGIONAL WORKS OFFICER

GENERAL CHARACTERISTICS

The Regional Works Officer provides a single point of contact on behalf of the works professions with the user or client professions. He provides advice to the Regional Team of Officers and the RHA on works matters and is responsible for the architectural, engineering and surveying aspects of all building, engineering, maintenance and property management matters in the Region.

PRINCIPAL RESPONSIBILITIES

1. Participates in the Regional Team of Officers' preparation of planning guidelines, review of AHA plans and preparation of RHA plans.

2. Ensures that the RHA and Regional Team of Officers are aware of the works implications of plans.

3. Translates the client's brief into plans for the delivery of capital works.

4. Arranges for the design and construction of all planned capital works.

5. Recommends to the RHA the new building works to be delegated to AHAs.

6. Maintains the professional and technical standards of building, engineering and property management throughout the Region and within each of its Areas, by monitoring and co-ordinating Area works staff.

7. Reviews and approves AHA maintenance budgets.

WORKING RELATIONSHIPS

Accountable to: Regional Health Authority
Manages: Regional Architect
                               Regional Engineer
                               Regional Quantity Surveyor.

Monitors and co-ordinates: Area Works Officers
Member of the Regional Team of
   Officers.

DISTRICT FINANCE OFFICER

GENERAL CHARACTERISTICS

The District Finance Officer provides financial advice to the DMT and to the individual senior managers within the District. He is responsible for any financial services which the Area Treasurer requires to be carried out by District finance staff. He co-ordinates preparation of the District budget. In addition, he is responsible for ensuring that all existing services or new proposals are subjected to critical financial appraisal, with a view to achieving an effective use of resources.

PRINCIPAL RESPONSIBILITIES

1. **Provides financial advice to DMT**

    1.1 Advises and co-ordinates the DMT on financial aspects of its work.
      1.1.1 Advises on the financing of planning proposals for the District.
      1.1.2 Monitors the District's expenditure in relation to budget and draws deviations to the attention of the DMT.
      1.1.3 Monitors the District's use of resources in relation to the service provided and identifies opportunities for improvement.

    1.2 Advises and co-ordinates individual managers within the District on financial aspects of their work. In particular:
      1.2.1 Assists them to prepare their own budgets.
      1.2.2 Monitors their expenditure and use of resources and advises them on improvements.

2. **Provides financial services**

    Provides financial services as required by the Area Treasurer.

3. **Co-ordinates preparation of the District budget**

    Ensures that budgets for District services are prepared, within allocations and in accordance with the District plan.

4. **Monitors the effective use of resources**

    Ensures that officers have adequate information by which to achieve economy, efficiency and the effective use of resources. Ensures that where value for money is not being obtained, or where there is unnecessary waste, those responsible are made aware of the fact.

WORKING RELATIONSHIPS

Accountable to: Area Health Authority
Manages: Subordinate finance staff at District
Monitored and co-ordinated by: The Area Treasurer, under whose direction he provides financial services as required.
Member of the District Management Team.

AREA TREASURER

GENERAL CHARACTERISTICS

The Area Treasurer provides financial advice to the AHA, including the Family Practitioner Committee, to the Area Team of Officers, of which he is a member, and to the individual senior managers of the Authority. He is responsible for providing all the financial services required for the AHA's operations, including those under the control of officers of Districts, and for monitoring and co-ordinating the work of the District Finance Officers. He co-ordinates preparation of the Area budget and ensures that all existing schemes or new proposals are on sound financial lines, having particular regard to the effective use of resources.

PRINCIPAL RESPONSIBILITIES

1. **Provides financial advice to the AHA and its officers**

   1.1 Advises the AHA itself and the FPC on the financial implications of policy issues, and draws to their attention any financial matters that warrant notice.

   1.2 Advises and co-ordinates the Area Team of Officers on financial aspects of its work.*

       1.2.1 Assists the team on the allocation of resources to Districts and the preparation of planning guidelines.

       1.2.2 Assists in the review and approval of District plans.

       1.2.3 Monitors Districts' expenditure in relation to their budgets and draws deviations to the attention of the DMT concerned and, if necessary, to the Area Team of Officers.

       1.2.4 Monitors Districts' use of resources in relation to the service provided and identifies opportunities for improvement.

       1.2.5 Advises the Area Team of Officers on the preparation of the AHA's capital programme and on the financial implications of planning proposals.

       1.2.6 Assists in the preparation of the consolidated Area plan and in the preparation of the budget for the AHA's own operations, including those of the FPC.

   1.3 Provides financial advice to senior officers of the AHA. In particular:

       1.3.1 Assists them to prepare their budgets.

       1.3.2 Monitors their expenditure and use of resources.

2. **Provides financial services to the AHA**

   2.1 Provides all financial services needed for the AHA's own operations, including those under the control of the FPC and of officers of Districts. In particular:

---

* In Areas not divided into Districts, the next four tasks listed below will refer to the Area's own plan and to its own expenditure and use of resources.

143

2.1.1 Devises and implements internal financial control systems, including a financial management and internal audit system.

2.1.2 Keeps all necessary financial records and accounts.

2.1.3 Provides for the computation and payment of wages and salaries, for the payment of accounts, and for the custody and disbursement of the Authority's funds, including cash.

2.1.4 Provides financial information to the RHA, to the AHA and to the Area Team of Officers, e.g. on income and expenditure in relation to budget.

2.2 At his discretion, delegates part of this work to the District Finance Officer.

2.3 Monitors District finance functions and, in particular, specifies financial policies and procedures to be observed and services to be provided by District Finance Officers. Monitors and, where necessary, co-ordinates the work of District Finance Officers, to ensure that Area financial policies are being adhered to and that delegated financial services are being properly carried out.

3. **Co-ordinates the preparation of the Area budget**

Ensures that budgets for Area services and for Districts are prepared, within allocations and in accordance with Area plans.

WORKING RELATIONS

Accountable to: Area Health Authority
Manages: Area finance department staff
Monitors and co-ordinates: District Finance Officers
Monitored and co-ordinated by: Regional Treasurer.
Member of the Area Team of Officers.

REGIONAL TREASURER

GENERAL CHARACTERISTICS

The Regional Treasurer provides financial advice to the RHA, to the Regional Team of Officers, of which he is a member, and to the senior managers of the Authority. In addition he provides all the financial services required for the RHA's own operations. He is head of his profession within the Region and monitors and co-ordinates the work of the Area finance functions. He co-ordinates the preparation of the Regional budget.

PRINCIPAL RESPONSIBILITIES

1. **Provides financial advice to the RHA and its officers**

    1.1 Advises the RHA itself on the financial implications of policy issues, and draws to its attention any financial matters that warrant its notice.

    1.2 Advises and co-ordinates the Regional Team of Officers on financial aspects of their work.

    1.2.1 Assists in allocation of resources to the AHAs and prepares planning guidelines.

    1.2.2 Assists in the review and approval of planning proposals.

    1.2.3 Monitors AHA's income and expenditure in relation to their budgets and draws deviations to the attention of the AHA concerned and, if necessary, to the Regional Team of Officers.

    1.2.4 Monitors AHAs' use of resources in relation to the service provided and identifies opportunities for improvement.

    1.2.5 Advises the Regional Team of Officers on the preparation of the RHA's capital programme and scrutinises individual projects from the financial standpoint.

    1.2.6 Assists in the preparation of the consolidated Regional plan and the preparation of the budget for the RHA's own operations.

    1.3 Advises and co-ordinates senior officers of the RHA on financial aspects of their work. In particular:

    1.3.1 Assists them to prepare their budgets.

    1.3.2 Monitors their expenditure and use of resources.

2. **Provides financial services to the RHA**

    2.1 Provides all financial services needed for the RHA's own operations. In particular:

    2.1.1 Devises and implements internal financial control systems, including financial management and internal audit systems.

    2.1.2 Keeps all necessary financial records and accounts.

    2.1.3 Provides for the computation and payment of wages and

145

salaries, for the payment of accounts, and for the custody and disbursement of the Authority's funds, including cash.

    2.1.4 Provides financial information to the DHSS, to the RHA and to the Regional Team of Officers, e.g. on income and expenditure in relation to budget.

3. Monitors Area finance functions

In particular, as head of his profession within the Region, monitors and, where necessary, co-ordinates the work of the Area Treasurers to ensure that they adhere to NHS financial policies and procedures.

4. Co-ordinates preparation of Regional budget

Ensures that the budgets for the Areas and for the Regional services are prepared, within allocations and in accordance with Regional plans.

WORKING RELATIONSHIPS

Accountable to: Regional Health Authority
Manages: Regional finance department staff
Monitors and co-ordinates: Area Treasurers
Member of the Regional Team of Officers.

146

DISTRICT ADMINISTRATOR

GENERAL CHARACTERISTICS

The District Administrator is accountable to the AHA for the management of institutional support services. He provides certain administrative support services to his DMT colleagues, including personnel services, planning assistance and management services, where a District is large enough to justify separate provision. He provides general administrative co-ordination of the work of the DMT. As a member of the DMT, he is jointly responsible (with other members of the team) for the functions delegated to the DMT by the AHA.

PRINCIPAL RESPONSIBILITIES

1. **Manages institutional and support services** (including catering, domestic, laundry, CSSD, medical records and stores, and grounds maintenance services) required by clinics, health centres, hospitals and other service property in the District. He is responsible for accommodation, secretarial and office services for District staff and clinicians (excluding family practitioners). For each service he:

    1.1 Recommends the necessary management organisation and agrees it with the Area Administrator,* keeps it continually under review and proposes changes as necessary.

    1.2 Develops plans to improve levels of service or reduce costs for all these services, in close collaboration with his subordinates, and determines priorities between plans for different services.

    1.3 Initiates discussion within the DMT on District plans for institutional and support services.

    1.4 Keeps revenue expenditure and staffing levels and gradings in line with agreed budgets and plans.

    1.5 Monitors performance of his subordinate managers responsible for these services and initiates corrective action as necessary.

    1.6 Exercises operational control of building and engineering staff, for activities within the District maintenance budget. These staff will be accountable professionally and technically to the Area Works Officer.

2. **Provides administrative support services as required.** The administrative support services needed will vary from District to District, and in many cases will be provided from the Area. The AHA will decide, after consultation with Area officers and the DMT, which of the following services need to be provided locally by the District Administrator:

    2.1 Personnel services. These involve assisting managers with local recruitment and publicity effort, employment of administrative and clerical staff, induction and orientation courses, job evaluation and implementation of productivity schemes.

---

* In some Areas, certain services, e.g. CSSD and laundry, will be provided on an Area basis.

2.2 Management services, such as work study.

2.3 Planning assistance to District health-care planning teams.

2.4 Public and press relations. The District Administrator will often be the link between the DMT and the Community Health Council, local voluntary bodies and the press, and he co-ordinates initial action on complaints from the public (except where family practitioners are concerned).

3. **Sees that District institutional services are co-ordinated** with medical, para-medical and nursing services and with services provided direct from AHA or RHA, e.g. capital building and ambulance services.

4. **Provides general administrative co-ordination of the work of the DMT.**

4.1 Co-ordinates and participates in the preparation by the DMT of an overall District plan and budget proposals for discussion with the Area Team of Officers and presentation to the AHA.

4.2 Arranges for members of the DMT to be provided with the necessary staff assistance to draw up their individual aspects of the District Plan.

4.3 Arranges for the individual plans to be presented to the team.

4.4 Identifies, with his colleagues, the major planning issues involved and presents conflicting claims for resources, so that the team can together make an objective appraisal of priorities within the resources available.

4.5 Notifies other officers who are not members of the DMT when topics of concern to them are to be discussed, and sees that they receive agendas, papers, etc.

4.6 Prepares the team's agreed proposals and options for discussion with the Area Team of Officers and subsequently for presentation to the AHA.

4.7 Prepares a regular progress report for the AHA on major problems facing the District in the implementation of agreed plans and on the steps to be taken to resolve them. This report will represent the consensus view of the team as a whole but will include individual reports, as necessary, from individual members of the team.

4.8 **Provides a channel of communication for the team.**

4.8.1 Attends meetings of the AHA as appropriate to assist the DMT Chairman present the team's agreed advice on policy plans and budget proposals and to discuss the team's progress report.

4.8.2 Attends meetings of the AHA, with members of the DMT, when matters critical to the District are to be discussed.

4.8.3 Acts as the formal channel of communication for the DMT.

WORKING RELATIONSHIPS

Accountable to:	Area Health Authority
Manages:	Support Services Manager
	General Administrator
	Sector Administrators.
Exercises operational control over:	Works officers (in respect of maintenance functions in the District budget)
Monitored and co-ordinated by:	Area Administrator

Member of the District Management Team.

DISTRICT SUPPORT SERVICES MANAGER

GENERAL CHARACTERISTICS

The Support Services Manager manages the catering, domestic, laundry, personal transport, CSSD, stores and medical records (except FPC records) services, and exercises operational control over maintenance services, within the District. These can account for up to 20 percent of total District revenue costs. He is accountable to the District Administrator.

PRINCIPAL RESPONSIBILITIES

1. **Recommends organisation, staffing levels and expenditure for each service of which he is the manager,** and keeps these constantly under review, proposing changes as necessary.

   1.1 Develops details of management organisation and establishment for discussion with the District Administrator.

   1.2 Participates in the selection of immediate subordinates and of staff one rank below them.

   1.3 Allocates responsibilities to his subordinates and prepares, agrees with the officer concerned, and updates annually as necessary, role specifications for all officers above first-line supervision.

2. **Prepares annual plans for the development of institutional and support services within the District,** working with his immediate subordinates and with health-care planning teams.

   2.1 Familiarises himself with existing District plans and with proposals affecting institutional services being evolved by health-care planning teams.

   2.2 Identifies major problems or opportunities to improve support services, reduce costs or redeploy existing resources to better effect, and formulates detailed action programmes to solve the problems or realise the opportunities.

   2.3 Translates the action programmes into staffing levels and budgets and determines the priorities between competing programmes in line with guidelines established by the DMT.

   2.4 Formulates an annual District institutional services plan, that reflects accepted health-care planning team proposals and includes any changes to management organisation and staffing levels in the services concerned.

   2.5 Participates in DMT discussions affecting institutional services and adjusts plans as agreed.

3. **Secures implementation of agreed plans.**

   3.1 Establishes clear performance targets for his subordinates and ensures that they are familiar with agreed District plans.

149

3.2 Monitors the performance of his subordinate managers in implementing agreed plans and sees that expenditure on individual services
remains in line with agreed budgets.

3.3 Identifies the need for corrective action, discusses this, as necessary,
with the officer concerned, with the District Administrator and with
the DMT.

WORKING RELATIONSHIPS

Accountable to: District Administrator
Manages: Sector Administrators*
                       Catering Officer
                       Domestic Services Officer
                       Stores, Supplies and Transport Officer
                       Laundry Manager
                       CSSD Officer.

---

* In some Districts these may be directly subordinate to the District Administrator and they
may be the managers of some institutional services staff, e.g. kitchen staff, domestics and
porters.

SECTOR ADMINISTRATOR

GENERAL CHARACTERISTICS

The Sector Administrator co-ordinates the various administrative support services in the hospitals, health centres and clinics in his sector with each other, and he ensures that they combine effectively with doctors, nurses, paramedical and social services staff working in the sector.

PRINCIPAL RESPONSIBILITIES

1. **Monitors and co-ordinates, and in some cases* manages directly, institutional support services in his sector**

   1.1 Maintains medical records and financial records and pays wages and salaries, as necessary.
   1.2 Carries out certain personnel functions for all staff, other than nursing or medical staff, including the maintenance of all personnel records.
   1.3 Provides typing and office services.
   1.4 Purchases and stores supplies and equipment.
   1.5 Provides catering, laundry and CSSD services, where these are not made available on a District or Area-wide basis.
   1.6 Provides personal transport for sector staff and takes responsibility for administration of staff accommodation in the sector.

2. **Sees that institutional services in the sector combine to meet the needs of patients and professional staff**

   2.1 Maintains contact with doctors (GPs and hospital doctors), nurses, paramedical and local social services staff in the sector to identify opportunities to improve institutional and support services.
   2.2 Contributes towards discussions within the sector on proposed changes in local services and takes necessary administrative action to implement agreed changes, e.g. to outpatient procedures, medical records systems.
   2.3 Provides a channel of communication between the District Administrator and professional staff.
   2.4 Keeps in touch with local voluntary organisations, local press, etc., to ensure that local health services are sensitive to local needs and that local people are well informed about their health services.
   2.5 Initiates action to deal with complaints and decides which complaints need to be referred to the District Administrator.

* Two basic alternative organisation patterns are possible for institutional services within Districts. Under the first alternative, the Sector Administrator manages all the support staff and is responsible for their budgets. Under the second, functional managers at District, e.g. catering and laundry manager, are responsible for the different services and, although they outpost staff to the sector, they remain responsible for the budget. Outposted staff, in this case, are subject to the monitoring and co-ordinating authority of the Sector Administrator.

3. **Participates, as appropriate, in District planning activities**
   3.1 Contributes to proposals for improving administrative services within the District.
   3.2 Participates in the work of health-care planning teams where he has a particular interest.
   3.3 Participates, as appropriate, in the work of planning and commissioning teams for new buildings in the sector.

WORKING RELATIONSHIPS

Accountable to: *either* District Administrator
                             or Support Services Manager
Manages: Sector administrative staff not outposted by District functional managers (e.g. Catering Officer)
Monitors and co-ordinates: Administrative staff outposted from District.

152

AREA ADMINISTRATOR

GENERAL CHARACTERISTICS

The Area Administrator is the Secretary to the Area Health Authority. In addition, he is directly accountable to the Authority for the management of administrative services provided by the Area and for the general administrative co-ordination of the Area Team of Officers. As a member of the team, he is jointly responsible with the other members of the team for the functions delegated to it by the AHA.

PRINCIPAL RESPONSIBILITIES

1. **As secretary to the AHA**

   1.1 Acts as a formal channel of communication with the DHSS, RHAs, AHAs and outside bodies, and maintains contact with neighbouring Areas and local authorities.

   1.2 Provides secretariat services to the AHA, the FPC and officer committees and professional advisory committees, as required.

   1.3 Identifies opportunities and presents proposals to the Area Team of Officers for improving organisation and administration within the Area generally.

   1.4 Provides (jointly with the local authority) secretariat support needed to promote the effectiveness of machinery for collaboration between the AHA and the coterminous local authority, maintains contact with his counterpart in local government and ensures that plans agreed with the local authority are successfully implemented.

   1.5 Sees that appropriate officers represent the AHA as necessary in meetings with outside bodies, e.g. meetings of Area joint consultative committees.

   1.6 Ensures that the FPC is consulted when Area plans are being developed and that its views are taken into account.

2. **Manages Area administrative services**

   2.1 Prepares and presents to the AHA plans for the development of administrative services provided by the Area, and controls performance of subordinate managers in implementing agreed plans and policies. These services will normally include support services for the FPC, ambulance services, personnel services, management services, and supplies.

   2.2 Prepares regular progress reviews for the AHA, showing progress in implementing agreed plans and recommending corrective action where necessary.

   2.3 Identifies the implications of DHSS and RHA policies for Area administrative services and recommends action to be taken by the AHA.

153

2.4 Maintains contact with the RHA, and participates in the formulation of Regional policy and guidance on administrative matters.

2.5 Maintains and develops the professional standards of all administrative staff within the Area, and in particular promotes multi-disciplinary management development programmes.

2.6 Arranges for the handling of complaints at Area level and for action to be taken in emergency situations; identifies the need for legal advice and briefs the Regional legal adviser.

2.7 Provides general administrative support for AHA staff, including accommodation and office services.

3. **Provides general administrative co-ordination of the work of the Area Team of Officers**

3.1 Sees that appropriate planning guidelines for each DMT are formulated, agreed by the Area Officers concerned, and issued.

3.2 Co-ordinates and participates in the critical review of DMT plans and in the monitoring of DMT performance in implementing agreed plans and policies.

3.3 Co-ordinates and participates in the preparation of the overall Area plan and budget, for approval by the AHA and submission to the RHA.

    3.3.1 Arranges for the Area Team of Officers and individual members of it to be provided with the necessary administrative staff assistance to draw up plans for Area services.

    3.3.2 Arranges for the presentation of planning proposals, coming both from DMTs and from other Area officers, to the team.

    3.3.3 Helps identify the major planning issues involved and presents conflicting or competing claims for resources, so that the team can together make an objective appraisal of priorities within available resources.

    3.3.4 Following team discussion, prepares a draft of a plan for agreement with the team and presentation to the AHA.

3.4 Prepares a regular progress review for the Area Team of Officers and the AHA, setting out progress in implementing agreed plans and suggesting action to be taken, agreed as necessary with other team members, to correct any shortfall.

WORKING RELATIONSHIPS

Accountable to:	Area Health Authority
Manages:	AHA Secretariat
	Administrator (Family Practitioner Services)
	General Administrator
	Area Chief Ambulance Officer
	Area Personnel Officer
	Area Supplies Officer
	Area Management Services Officer

154

Monitored and co-ordinated by: Regional Administrator
Monitors and co-ordinates: District Administrators
Co-ordinates: AHA direct-appointees e.g. Area Works
Officer, Area Pharmaceutical Officer.
Member of Area Team of Officers.

ADMINISTRATOR (FAMILY PRACTITIONER SERVICES)

GENERAL CHARACTERISTICS

The Administrator (Family Practitioner Services) will provide the AHA with the views of the Family Practitioner Committee (FPC) on all matters relevant to Area policies and plans, and he will advise the FPC of relevant AHA policies and plans and of their implications. He acts as the formal link with the Medical Practices Committee and the DHSS, and provides general secretariat services and advice to the FPC and its committees. In addition, the Administrator advises the FPC and individual contractors on particular problems. He receives complaints and conducts necessary administrative and conciliation procedures.

PRINCIPAL RESPONSIBILITIES

1. **Informs Area and District staff of the FPC's views and proposals,** particularly on the planning and development of health centres, on attachment schemes and on manpower planning, and advises, assists and supports the AHA in the general planning process.

2. **Ensures that the FPC is informed of AHA plans** in general and, in particular, of any AHA policies on the planning and organisation of the family practitioner services, manpower planning and all other relevant developments, including proposals for health centres and attachment schemes. Advises the FPC on the implications of AHA policies generally, and on any administrative action required.

    2.1 Acts as administrative link between the FPC, the Medical Practices Committee and the DHSS in relation to the offering of contracts for general medical services.
    2.2 Undertakes surveys of general medical practice manpower for the Medical Practices Committee.
    2.3 Advertises medical practice vacancies and arranges related interviewing and selection procedures.

3. **Provides general secretariat services and advice to the FPC and its committees.**

    3.1 Monitors the performance of senior FPC staff.
    3.2 Provides secretariat services to the FPC and its committees and maintains contact with local representative family practitioner committees.
    3.3 Advises the FPC and its committees on relevant provisions of Acts, Regulations and terms of service of independent contractors.
    3.4 Maintains and publishes professional lists of contractors, processes applications for admission and withdrawal, and updates necessary records, including prime records relating to payments to contractors and registers of patients on lists of general medical practitioners.
    3.5 Authorises payments to contractors and sees that these are made promptly.

3.6 Maintains surveillance of the adequacy of family practitioner services and advises the FPC on the classification of medical practice areas.

4. **Advises on problems relating to individual contractors.**

4.1 Advises family practitioners on all matters relating to their terms of service and conditions of remuneration, including advice about changes in the organisation of medical practices e.g. engagement of partners and assistants and formation of group practices.

4.2 Advises medical practitioners on the employment of ancillary staff and the reimbursement of their salaries, on the acceptability of proposals on practice premises in connection with the reimbursement of rent and rates, the making of improvement grants and Finance Corporation loans. Arranges for the inspection of premises, where necessary, and advises the FPC on all such applications.

4.3 Advises general medical and dental practitioners and other contractors on the legal and financial implications of health centre practice in relation to their terms of service and conditions of remuneration.

4.4 Consults individual practitioners on the programme layout and design of health centres.

4.5 Negotiates the legal and financial terms upon which family practitioners are to work in health centres.

4.6 Receives complaints against family practitioners and contractors; undertakes administrative conciliation; processes complaints requiring formal investigation; advises complaints and respondents of Regulations and procedure; prepares service committee reports and represents the FPC at appeals and hearings, as required.

5. Prepares and publishes rota arrangements for pharmaceutical services.

6. Administers scheme for testing of drugs and appliances.

WORKING RELATIONSHIPS

Accountable to: Area Administrator
Manages: FPC staff, including attached AHA finance staff.

AREA PERSONNEL OFFICER

GENERAL CHARACTERISTICS

Individual officers of the AHA are responsible for the personnel management of their subordinates. The Area Personnel Officer assists managers to develop and implement sound personnel policies, so that the Service continues to be able to attract and retain sufficient staff of the required calibre, and to help ensure that the best possible use is made of scarce resources.

PRINCIPAL RESPONSIBILITIES

1. **Assists managers to develop organisational structures and to control establishment levels, to meet the needs of the Service and the staff concerned**

   1.1 Advises on organisational arrangements and ensures that they are in line with AHA organisational and operating policies.

   1.2 Sees that role specifications are prepared and agreed for all senior staff and are periodically reviewed. Specifies vacancies for recruitment and selection purposes.

   1.3 Assists in the identification of needs for changes in the organisational structure.

2. **Assists in the local recruitment effort**

   2.1 Assists managers to forecast their future manpower needs, where this is likely to be a critical factor.

   2.2 Provides publicity about Health Service careers and gives information and advice to those enquiring about non-nursing posts.

   2.3 Co-ordinates advertising activity in the AHA and collects and disseminates information about the cost and effectiveness of advertising media.

   2.4 Maintains contact with the Department of Employment, local authority careers officers, local schools and further education establishments about employment opportunities in the AHA.

   2.5 Helps develop local selection procedures within national and Regional guidelines, and assists, as requested, in assessment of candidates.

3. **Supports line managers in developing the managerial skills of their staffs**

   3.1 Formulates staff appraisal procedures, within national guidelines, for agreement with the managers concerned, and helps develop and implement staff record systems.

   3.2 Assists the various professional and departmental heads to identify the management training needs of their staff and to develop and implement programmes for meeting them.

   3.3 Assists with training programmes, including induction courses and in-service training.

4. **Advises managers on personnel policy questions generally**

    4.1 Maintains contact with RHA personnel officers and contributes to Regional personnel policies.

    4.2 Co-ordinates distribution of Whitley Council circulars and RHA personnel policy statements and, where action is required, brings this to the attention of the managers concerned.

    4.3 Advises the Area Team of Officers on its response to DMT proposals for changing the organisation and grading or establishment levels.

    4.4 Provides advice on implementation of productivity schemes and keeps in touch with national developments in this field, e.g. identifies successful schemes so that managers can visit the units involved to evaluate them for themselves.

    4.5 Identifies the local implications of any new legislation affecting industrial relations and advises managers on steps to take, e.g. to meet the requirements of the Industrial Relations Act.

5. **Helps ensure that general conditions of work are suitable**

    5.1 Brings to the attention of line managers throughout the Area changes in general personnel policies and guidance issued by the DHSS.

    5.2 Develops consultative arrangements, including those for staff wishing to bring matters to the attention of senior managers, and advises AHA and District staff on steps to take in the event of disputes with staff.

    5.3 Maintains contact with the Factories' Inspectorate and takes initiating action to secure implementation of recommendations in their reports.

    5.4 Edits AHA staff newsletter and runs any staff suggestion schemes and social clubs.

    5.5 Provides administrative support to the occupational health service.

6. **Provides administrative support on personnel matters**

    6.1 Co-ordinates action on returns requested by the DHSS on personnel questions.

    6.2 Undertakes the formalities of appointment arrangements.

    6.3 Advises the AHA Administrator whether to propose to the RHA any variation from nationally-negotiated pay scales, within guidelines established by the DHSS.

WORKING RELATIONSHIPS

Accountable to:	Area Administrator
Manages:	Area personnel staff
Monitored by:	Regional Personnel Officer
Monitors and co-ordinates:	Attached District personnel staff.

AREA SUPPLIES OFFICER

GENERAL CHARACTERISTICS

The Area Supplies Officer ensures the provision of supplies support services to the AHA and to its constituent DMTs, within policies and procedures laid down by the DHSS and the RHA. For items to be purchased at AHA level, he obtains and communicates technical advice on specifications, forms of contract methods of ordering and quality control. He arranges storage and, where necessary, operates condemning procedures and disposes of stores. He also arranges the supply of equipment and furniture for new building undertaken by the Area works organisation.

PRINCIPAL RESPONSIBILITIES

1. **Formulates Area supplies policies and operating procedures**

   1.1 Advises the AHA on the interpretation of DHSS and Regional supplies policy and the formulation of Area supplies policy.

   1.2 Determines commodities that will be purchased, stored and distributed from Area, in consultation with District Administrators.

   1.3 Advises and prepares technical specification of items of supply other than drugs, medical and surgical equipment, works stores, and supplies provided under central or Regional contract.

   1.4 Reviews the storage resources of the Area and proposes location of Area stores.

   1.5 Sees that all storekeepers in the Area understand the format and processes of stores documentation and procedures for losses, conversion, repair, condemnation and disposal of goods.

2. **Manages Area supplies services for all goods that will be supplied from Area**

   2.1 Determines forms of contract for purchase of goods and supplies.

   2.2 Lists selected suppliers.

   2.3 Invites or evaluates tenders or negotiates, where appropriate, for supplies purchased under Area contracts, and co-ordinates activities of purchasing department.

   2.4 Provides or ensures arrangements for quality control of supplies.

   2.5 Determines stock levels and re-order points.

   2.6 Acquires equipment and furniture for all new buildings, where responsibility has been delegated to the AHA.

   2.7 Ensures appropriate arrangements for receipt, maintenance and distribution of supplies within the Area.

   2.8 Manages Area supplies staff. Monitors performance of his immediate subordinates and sees that AHA supplies procedures are followed in all stores.

3. **Monitors effectiveness of District supplies arrangements and provides professional leadership to supplies staff working within the Area**

   3.1 Advises on technical and professional questions.
   3.2 Identifies training and career development needs, working with the Area Personnel Officer.
   3.3 Assists in selection of stores staff in the Districts within the Area.
   3.4 Reviews statistical information on the supplies service in the Area and visits Area stores, etc. Identifies problems and recommends action required to the Area Administrator.

WORKING RELATIONSHIPS

Accountable to:	Area Administrator
Manages:	Assistant Area supplies officers
	Area storekeeper(s)
Monitored by:	Regional Supplies Officer
Monitors and co-ordinates:	District supplies and stores staff.

REGIONAL ADMINISTRATOR

GENERAL CHARACTERISTICS

The Regional Administrator is the Secretary to the Regional Health Authority. In addition, he is directly accountable to the Authority for the management of administrative services provided by the Region and for the general administrative co-ordination of the Regional Team of Officers. As a member of the team, he is jointly responsible with the other members for the functions delegated to them by the RHA.

PRINCIPAL RESPONSIBILITIES

1. Is Secretary to the RHA

1.1 Acts as a formal channel of communication with the DHSS, AHAs and outside bodies, and maintains contact with other Regions.

1.2 Provides secretariat services to the RHA and its committees, including officer committees and professional advisory committees.

1.3 Together with his colleagues on the Regional Team of Officers, identifies opportunities and presents proposals to improve the organisation of administration within the Region generally.

1.4 Sees that appropriate officers represent the RHA in meetings with outside bodies, e.g. meetings of Area joint consultative committees.

2. Manages Regional administrative services

2.1 Prepares and presents to the RHA, plans for the development of administrative services provided by the Region, and controls performance of subordinate managers in implementing agreed plans. These services include ambulance services, personnel services, management services, information services, supplies and public relations.

2.2 Prepares regular progress reviews for the Authority, showing progress in implementing agreed plans and recommending corrective action where necessary.

2.3 Identifies the implications of DHSS policies for Regional administrative services and recommends action to be taken by the RHA.

2.4 Maintains contact with the DHSS and participates in the formulation of national policy and guidance.

2.5 Maintains and develops the professional standards of all administrative staff within the Region, and particularly promotes multi-disciplinary management development programmes.

2.6 Arranges for the handling of complaints at Regional level and for action to be taken in emergency situations, and arranges for the provision of legal services.

2.7 Provides general administrative support to RHA staff, including accommodation and office services.

3. Co-ordinates the work of the Regional Team of Officers

3.1 Sees that appropriate planning guidelines for AHAs are formulated, agreed by the Regional officers concerned, and issued.

3.2 Co-ordinates and participates in the critical review of AHA plans and in the monitoring of AHA performance in implementing agreed plans and Regional policies.

3.3 Co-ordinates and participates in the preparation of an overall Regional plan and budget, for approval by the RHA and submission to the DHSS.

    3.3.1 Arranges for the team, and individual members of it, to be provided with the necessary staff assistance to draw up plans for Regional services.

    3.3.2 Arranges for the presentation to the team of planning proposals, both for the development of services and for capital building (coming both from the Region and from AHAs).

    3.3.3 Identifies the major planning issues involved and presents conflicting or competing claims for resources, so that the team can make an objective appraisal of priorities, within available resources.

    3.3.4 Following team discussion, prepares a draft of a Regional health services plan and its associated capital building programme, for agreement with the team and presentation to the RHA.

3.4 Prepares a regular progress review for the Regional Team of Officers and the RHA, setting out progress in implementing agreed plans and suggesting action to be taken, agreed as necessary with other members of the team, to correct any problems arising.

WORKING RELATIONSHIPS

Accountable to: Regional Health Authority

Manages: RHA Secretariat (including Public Relations Officer)
Regional Personnel Officer
Regional Supplies Officer
Regional Management Services Officer
Administrator (Services Planning)
Administrator (Capital Building Programme)
Regional Ambulance Officer

Monitors and co-ordinates: Legal Adviser
Area Administrators

Member of the Regional Team of Officers.

REGIONAL SUPPLIES OFFICER

GENERAL CHARACTERISTICS

The Regional Supplies Officer advises the RHA on the appropriate policies and organisation of the supplies function within the Region. He establishes quality control procedures and issues advice and guidance on supplies questions to AHA staff. He promotes rationalisation of supplies and equipment, and for certain items (to be agreed with AHAs) prepares specifications and negotiates terms. In certain cases he arranges storage and distribution of stocks direct to users.

PRINCIPAL RESPONSIBILITIES

1. Advises on the policies and organisation of the Regional supplies function

1.1 Maintains contact with the DHSS and contributes to national supplies policies.

1.2 Advises the Authority on action to be taken on DHSS supplies policies.

1.3 Proposes an organisational structure for the supplies function in the Region and for the allocation of responsibilities between the RHA and its AHAs.

1.4 Makes recommendations about the location of stores throughout the Region.

1.5 In accordance with standing financial regulations, establishes procedures for conversion or repair, condemnation or disposal of goods and operates losses procedures.

1.6 Assists the Regional Team of Officers to monitor the performance of Area Supplies Officers in rationalising supplies and equipment, obtaining better value for money, improving the service and reducing costs. Identifies the need for intervention by the RHA and recommends the steps required.

2. Issues advice and guidance on supplies questions to Area Supplies Officers

2.1 Prepares technical specifications for major items of supplies other than drugs, medical and surgical equipment, works stores, and supplies provided under central, i.e. national, contract arrangements.

2.2 Determines forms of contract for purchase of goods and supplies, and advises AHAs on tendering and negotiating procedures and on the arrangements necessary to ensure that goods are of the required quality.

2.3 Establishes procedures covering maximum and minimum stock levels, safety stocks required, economic order quantities and ordering (or requisitioning) of goods from suppliers or Regional stores. Also establishes operating procedures for stores documentation.

3. **Manages Regional supplies services**

    3.1   Defines the items that will be purchased, stored and distributed from Regional stores. Lists selected suppliers, invites and evaluates tenders or negotiates, where appropriate, for supplies under Regional contract, and co-ordinates activities of purchasing department.

    3.2   Acquires equipment and furniture for all major new buildings not delegated to AHAs.

    3.3   Ensures appropriate arrangements for receipt, maintenance and distribution of items by the Regional supplies organisation.

    3.4   Provides professional leadership for AHA supplies staff. Identifies their training and career development needs, assists in staff selection, appraisal and disciplinary procedures.

WORKING RELATIONSHIPS

Accountable to:	Regional Administrator
Manages:	Assistant Regional supplies officers Regional storekeepers
Monitors:	Area Supplies Officers

REGIONAL PERSONNEL OFFICER

GENERAL CHARACTERISTICS

Individual RHA and AHA officers* are responsible for the personnel management of their staff. The Regional Personnel Officer undertakes certain manpower planning and establishment control functions for the Region as a whole. In the light of agreed Regional plans he provides advice on the recruitment, training, staff appraisal and career development of senior and middle managers in the Region, and promotes action to ensure that the skills of existing staff are developed and used.

PRINCIPAL RESPONSIBILITIES

1. **Undertakes Regional manpower planning and establishment control functions as a service to the Regional Team of Officers**

    1.1 Acts in consultation with Regional Medical Officer, Regional Nursing Officer, the Regional Manpower Committee and AHA staff in forecasting future requirements for selected staff e.g. consultants, paramedical and other staff in short supply, and in the evaluation of present age-distribution and wastage rates, to determine annual recruitment and training needs for the Region.

    1.2 Identifies posts in excess of current establishment levels and co-ordinates the manpower section of the annual Regional health plan for submission to the DHSS. Acts in consultation with professional staff in reviewing and evaluating all AHA proposals for changes to agreed establishment levels, grading and management organisation, and recommends RHA response.

    1.3 Submits requests for major changes in the agreed RHA staff organisation or for variations from agreed pay and condition of service, to the DHSS for approval.

    1.4 Within agreed guidelines and discretionary limits, reviews and approves variations from national pay scales and conditions of service, keeping the DHSS fully informed.

2. **Advises RHA and AHA managers on personnel management techniques and procedures**

    2.1 Provides advice and formulates RHA policy on recruitment sources and methods, selection techniques and induction procedures.

    2.2 Suggests staff appraisal and career counselling procedures, and helps to ensure that promising staff are identified and their training and career development needs are met.

    2.3 Issues guidance on the local implications of any new legislation affecting industrial relations and advises managers on steps to take e.g. to meet the requirements of the Industrial Relations Act.

* Including AHA officers working in Districts.

166

2.4 Brings to the attention of RHA managers and Area Personnel Officers changes in general or Regional personnel policies e.g. as a result of agreements reached in the Whitley Councils or guidance issued by the DHSS.

2.5 Provides advice on implementation of productivity schemes and keeps in touch with national developments in this field.

3. **Provides Regional training services, through a Regional training branch**

3.1 Provides services, as required, in support of professional training organised by statutory or other central bodies, e.g. CPGME.*

3.2 Identifies, in association with other Regional officers, training needs throughout the Region, proposes priorities and formulates plans for meeting priority needs.

3.3 Implements, or assists others to implement, training programmes for the Region, where Area or national or outside courses are inappropriate.

3.4 Collaborates with Colleges and Universities to which training responsibilities have been assigned.

3.5 Works closely with AHAs to assist them to develop suitable training programmes and implement them successfully.

4. **Assists the Regional Team of Officers to monitor AHA performance in implementing national and Regional personnel policies**

4.1 Reviews and evaluates AHA proposals on personnel matters, which will be included in AHA plans, and monitors performance in implementing recruitment and training programmes and measures to increase staff productivity.

4.2 Identifies any abnormally high wastage rates and helps the AHA personnel officer concerned to identify the reasons and propose corrective action.

4.3 Identifies the need for intervention by the RHA e.g. in the event of an industrial dispute, and proposes action to be taken.

4.4 Keeps the DHSS fully informed of major personnel problems and of reaction in the Region to any new personnel policy initiatives.

5. **Provides professional leadership to personnel officers throughout the Region**

5.1 Holds regular meetings with Area personnel officers and helps identify their training and career development needs.

5.2 Assists in selection of Area personnel officers.

WORKING RELATIONSHIPS

Accountable to: Regional Administrator

Manages: Regional personnel department staff

Monitors: Area Personnel Officers.

* Council for Postgraduate Medical Education.

ADMINISTRATOR (CAPITAL BUILDING PROGRAMME)

GENERAL CHARACTERISTICS

The Administrator (Capital Building Programme) co-ordinates the preparation of an annual Regional capital building plan, which in larger Regions will entail capital expenditure of up to £15 million a year, and exercises administrative control over the implementation of the agreed building programme to ensure that expenditure is kept within agreed budgets. He also acquires and disposes of land and buildings on behalf of the RHA.

PRINCIPAL RESPONSIBILITIES

1. **Co-ordinates the preparation of the annual Regional capital building plan, for consideration by the Regional Team of Officers**

   1.1 Works with service-planning teams to identify requirements for new buildings in the Region.

   1.2 Maintains contact with DHSS and sees that national building policy standards and guidance are taken into account in Regional building plans.

   1.3 Drafts, for consideration by the Regional Team of Officers, the capital building programme for the next 10 years, which;

   1.3.1 Takes into account Regional service plans.

   1.3.2 Specifies the projects to be undertaken in each Area, the content of each e.g. number of beds by specialty, the estimated capital cost and revenue consequences, and the approximate location.

   1.3.3 Proposes priorities between projects.

   1.3.4 Shows, in consultation with the finance function, how capital expenditure and consequential increases in revenue will be phased.

   1.3.5 Identifies major consequences for existing buildings e.g. hospital closures.

   1.4 Identifies projects that should be delegated to AHAs.

2. **Exercises administrative control over the agreed building programme**

   2.1 Co-ordinates action by the Regional Team of Officers to develop Regional building policies on, for example, standard designs, and to determine details of functional content and operational policies for each major project, including number of beds, number and location of theatres, ward layout policies, number of entrances and location of kitchens

   2.2 Manages project administrators and assists them to see that an adequate brief and co-ordinated work programme is prepared for each project. Helps them to ensure that drawings are processed as necessary through the DHSS, the RHA and the Regional Team of Officers, and that regular progress reviews for each project are prepared.

2.3 Adjusts the nature or phasing of projects as necessary, in the light of staffing and revenue consequences.

2.4 Assists the Regional Team of Officers to monitor capital expenditure against agreed budgets and suggests changes in phasing of projects as required.

3. Acquires and disposes of land and buildings

3.1 Identifies, in consultation with RHA works staff, land and buildings to be acquired or disposed of as a result of capital developments.

3.2 Consults with local planning authorities and statutory bodies as necessary.

3.3 Carries out the initial negotiations and acquisition etc., ensuring that national policies and procedures are agreed.

3.4 Sees that agreed national procedures are followed before hospitals are closed as a result of the capital development programme.

WORKING RELATIONSHIPS

Accountable to :   Regional Administrator

Manages: Project administrators.

ADMINISTRATOR (REGIONAL SERVICES PLANNING)

GENERAL CHARACTERISTICS

The Administrator (Regional Services Planning) enables the Regional Administrator to contribute as necessary to plans for the development of health services in the Region and provides administrative support to the service-planning teams. He assists the Regional Administrator to co-ordinate the work of the Regional Team of Officers and provides professional advice and support to AHA planning staff as required.

PRINCIPAL RESPONSIBILITIES

1. **Secures the administrative contribution to plans for the development of health services in the Region**

   1.1 Recommends the number and type of administrative staff required, allocates planning assistants to service-planning teams and monitors their performance.

   1.2 Maintains contact with the DHSS and keeps planning assistants familiar with national policies, priorities and guidelines.

   1.3 Helps identify management information needs of service-planning teams and, in liaison with the Regional Medical Officer and his staff, helps develop a management information system.

   1.4 Monitors progress of service planning and takes steps (usually informally but, if necessary, through the Regional Medical Officer and the Regional Team of Officers) to ensure that individual service plans are developed on time, contain the required information and have been the subject of the necessary consultations.

   1.5 Represents the RHA, as required by the Regional Team of Officers, on joint planning bodies with local authorities.

   1.6 Manages services-planning assistants.

2. **Assists the Regional Administrator to co-ordinate the work of the Regional Team of Officers**

   2.1 Drafts annual planning guidelines for consideration by the team and issue to AHAs.

   2.2 Participates in reviews of Area health plans and, in particular, agrees with the AHA staff concerned any changes needed to the administrative elements of their plans.

   2.3 Provides whatever staff assistance is necessary to assist the team to develop a consolidated Regional health plan, including a capital building programme, on time and in the required format.

   2.4 Assists the team to monitor AHA performance in implementing agreed plans and participates as necessary in progress review meetings.

   2.5 Undertakes special planning studies as required by the team.

170

3. **Provides professional advice and support to AHA administrative planning staff**
   3.1 Interprets national and Regional policies to AHA staff as necessary.
   3.2 Familiarises himself with the latest techniques in service planning and keeps his colleagues fully informed of any major developments.
   3.3 Assists AHA staff as requested with particular planning problems.
   3.4 Helps identify the training and career development needs of RHA and AHA service-planning staff, and takes necessary steps to see that these are met.

WORKING RELATIONSHIPS

Accountable to: Regional Administrator

Manages: Services-planning assistants.

REGIONAL AMBULANCE OFFICER

GENERAL CHARACTERISTICS

The Regional Ambulance Officer advises the RHA on the organisation, development and control of ambulance services in the Region. On ambulance aid matters he provides this advice in consultation with the Regional Medical Officer. He ensures that AHAs plan for the development of ambulance services in close collaboration with each other. Finally, he may be directly responsible for the operational control of ambulance services in metropolitan districts in the Region.*

PRINCIPAL RESPONSIBILITIES

1. **Advises the RHA on the organisation, development and control of ambulance services in the Region**

   1.1 Provides professional advice on questions affecting the ambulance service.
   1.2 Contributes to national policy on the development of ambulance services, and identifies implications for the Region's ambulance service of national policies and guidance.
   1.3 Recommends minimum standards of service and common standards of equipment and controls e.g. vehicles and radio.
   1.4 Proposes allocation of planning and operational responsibilities to AHAs in cases of overlap i.e. where people in one Area look to another Area for inpatient services.
   1.5 Contributes to the development of Regional plans for action in the event of major accidents and other emergencies, including use of emergency reserve channels, and ensures that Area Chief Ambulance Officers understand their roles.

2. **Reviews and evaluates AHAs' plans for their ambulance services, to ensure that they are consistent with each other and collectively meet the Region's needs**

   2.1 Monitors performance of AHA ambulance services in implementing national and Regional policies and plans, including, where appropriate, links with local authorities.
   2.2 Proposes any special planning guidance on ambulance services which needs to be issued by the RHA to particular AHAs.
   2.3 Reviews and evaluates AHA plans for the development of ambulance services and recommends any changes required to the Regional Team of Officers.

---

* In some small Regions, the Chief Ambulance Officer of an AHA may be designated the Regional Ambulance Officer.

2.4 Determines, in collaboration with Area Chief Ambulance Officers, sites for ambulance stations and for the general deployment of ambulances.

2.5 Establishes and co-ordinates arrangements with neighbouring Regions in relation to the siting of ambulance stations adjacent to Regional boundaries, and in relation to the provision of operational services.

2.6 Co-ordinates, at RHA level, the preparation of briefs for the construction of capital buildings for the ambulance service.

3. **Secures necessary co-ordination between AHA ambulance services**

3.1 Develops, in conjunction with AHA ambulance officers, standing operating procedures that will ensure effective collaboration between different services, and holds regular meetings with Area Chief Ambulance Officers.

3.2 Secures effective emergency service cover and concentration of vehicle control arrangements at night and at weekends, throughout the Region.

3.3 Establishes, in collaboration with the Regional Supplies Officer, joint purchasing arrangements for new vehicles or equipment for all AHAs, and ensures appropriate arrangements for the maintenance and repair of vehicles.

3.4 Commissions and carries out special studies, as necessary, to identify and realise opportunities to improve ambulance services in the Region.

4. **Manages ambulance services for AHAs coterminous with metropolitan districts, and other AHAs too small to support economically an effective ambulance service. The Regional Ambulance Officer:**

4.1 Identifies those AHAs in the Region that are too small to support their own ambulance service and proposes arrangements for providing them with an adequate service.

4.2 Establishes a liaison committee, comprising representatives of the AHA served by the Regional Ambulance Service, the Regional Ambulance Officer and the Chief Ambulance Officer of the Metropolitan Ambulance Service.

4.3 Makes arrangements for operational control of ambulance services provided directly by the Region.

5. **Provides professional advice and leadership on questions affecting the ambulance service in the Region and, among other things:**

5.1 Ensures the provision of appropriate staff training arrangements, in collaboration with the Regional Medical Officer.

5.2 Takes the necessary steps, in collaboration with the Regional Medical Officer and the Regional Nursing Officer, to provide training facilities at Regional level, if these are not available locally i.e. at Area.

5.3 Advises AHA Chief Ambulance Officers on recruitment, training and career development questions.

5.4 Participates in the selection of senior ambulance staff within Areas.

WORKING RELATIONSHIPS

Accountable to: Regional Administrator

Manages: RHA ambulance staff

Monitors: Area Chief Ambulance Officers

Monitored by: Regional Medical Officer (medical aspects
                       only).

Printed in England for Her Majesty's Stationery Office by McCorquodale Printers Ltd.,
London.

HM 4821   Dd 502430   K480   8/72   McC 3309